THE BES
HAND

THE
BEST MAN'S
HANDBOOK

Henry Russell

DAVID & CHARLES
Newton Abbot   London

British Library Cataloguing in Publication Data
Russell, Henry
  The best man's handbook
  1. Weddings. Planning
  I. Title
  395'.22

  ISBN 0-7153-9314-0

First published 1990
Reprinted 1990

Line drawings by Peter Seaman

Printed in Great Britain
by Billings & Sons Ltd   Worcester
for David & Charles plc
Brunel House   Newton Abbot   Devon

CONTENTS

FOREWORD

DAVID: I should like you to be my Best Man.

JONATHAN: I should be honoured. (*Aside*) And also dead worried:
　So much to organise: the date;
Are Stag Night assignations quite the thing?
Are morning suits appropriate as rig?
Will I remember where I put the ring?
Are jokes about his old flames *infra dig*?
　I'd rather die than make him late!
(Exit in a panic)

If you have recently accepted the responsibility of being Best Man at a wedding and find yourself overwhelmed by feelings of unworthiness for the task, this book will put your mind at rest. The Best Man should be the Groom's secretary, valet and factotum, but there is no need to despair if you do not regard yourself as the living synthesis of James Boswell, Reginald Jeeves and Man Friday.

First, reassure yourself, remembering that you are not the first person to have submitted to such an ordeal. Think of the number of men who successfully perform the task every day — in 1987, the last year for which figures are available, there were 397,900 registered marriages in England and Wales, and it may safely be assumed that by no means all the Best Men at these were renaissance heroes.

The main sticking point for the Best Man is the speech which traditionally he is supposed to make at the reception. Yet there is no other occasion in human life at which a speech is required where everyone is rooting for the speaker. This book contains no model speeches; nor is it a repository of good jokes for the speech. There is, however, a great deal of material from newspaper stories and traditional sources; this has been included to provide ideas for the subject matter. The purpose of the book is inspirational, not prescriptive.

Finally, and perhaps most importantly, do not be intimidated by the tradition and etiquette of the whole wedding procedure. Remember that to every rule there are many exceptions, and almost nothing is indispensable. Within the limits of good taste and discretion outlined below, the best advice is: do what you like. With this as your guide, you can be the best Best Man.

I would like to thank the following for their midwifery in the birth of this book: Sara Jones (accessory before, during and after the fact); Richard Mawhinney (for starting the ball rolling); Chris Trevers and Patrick Scanlan (for keeping it in motion); Alun Williams (for making it possible); Rosalyn Wilkinson (some folklorist); Joy Meacham (Church House); Simon Bainbridge (*l'uomo singolare*); Tulip Noble; Isobel Munday; Sue Pearl.

I
WEDDINGS: THE STATE OF THE ART

As you stand at the foot of the aisle in a church or at the door of a register office, it is almost inevitable that you will feel intimidated by the pomp of the occasion. As the clergyman begins the weighty introduction to the marriage service — 'Dearly beloved, we are gathered together here in the sight of God, etc . . .' — your sense of awe may make you want to run away in panic. In such circumstances, it may relieve some of your anxiety to consider that, in historical terms, the ceremony is a parvenu. Although the practice of wedding comes from pre-Christian antiquity, the religious and civil trappings have developed comparatively recently: any two-thousand-year-old witness to the scene would shake his hoary locks and say with reason, 'Weddings are not what they used to be.'

In western civilisation, marriage began simply as the agreement of a man and a woman to live together. In Roman law, consent and cohabitation were of the essence and there were three forms of marriage. One, with great ceremony, numerous witnesses and animal sacrifices, was usually for patricians: this was called *confarreatio*. *Coemptio*, or marriage by purchase of the woman by the man, was used by plebians; but the commonest form was the plain *usus*, ie custom or practice. Religious ceremony was optional, an accesssorial matter designed to bring the wife under the authority of the husband. (Here, incidentally, lies the origin of our patrilineal tradition of the woman taking the man's surname.) Marriage could be dissolved by dissent alone.

So it remained until 1540, when the validity of *de facto* marriages was destroyed by an Act which provided that a formal marriage superseded

King Henry VIII, an early expert on marriage

any earlier informal one. Thereafter, the decrees of the Council of Trent (Trento in the Tyrol) in 1563 made a religious ceremony a practical necessity in all Catholic countries.

In those days, canon law forbade marriage between a Roman Catholic and a non-Roman Catholic except by dispensation from Rome. Such leave was only granted on receipt of an undertaking that all children of the union would be baptised, brought up and educated as Roman Catholics. This is no longer the case, although any individual priest may refuse to marry such a couple. The Roman Catholic Church still does not recognise any form of marriage other than its own.

However, during the 1530s King Henry VIII had broken with the Church of Rome, so these decrees had no force in English civil law. At this time, a frequent practice in England was for people to undertake 'half weddings'. These consisted of a wide variety of betrothal rites which were often as elaborate as a church ceremony. Many couples lived tally (cohabited without marriage), legitimising their relationship by gathering friends and kin to witness an exchange of rings or the jumping of a broom. ('Leaping the broomstick' was a Romany tradition: if the man touched the broom, he would be unfaithful; if the woman touched it, she was either not a virgin or already pregnant.)

Then in 1753, Lord Hardwicke's Act was passed with the object of making a ceremony essential to an English marriage. It became law on 25 March 1754 and it was thenceforth compulsory for all marriages to be recorded in a separate register, no longer in the same book as that used for births and deaths. Entries had to show the place of residence of both parties and their marital status, and had to be signed by two or more witnesses. All marriages were to be performed in church, the only exceptions to this rule being Jews and Quakers. Roman Catholics were not allowed their own ceremony until 1791. The minimum age for marriage with parental consent was fourteen for males, twelve for females, and so it remained until 1929, when it was raised to sixteen for both sexes.

Despite all this, long-established social custom resisted legislation to the extent that at the dawn of the nineteenth century perhaps as many as one in every three couples still lived together outside legal wedlock. The reasons for this were mainly economic — couples hoped to have a full church wedding when they cast off from their families and set up a separate home together. In the event, many could never afford to do so and their children were brought up in a communal home by parents and grandparents, uncles and aunts. In such cases a big wedding made no sense, either financially or as a symbol of independence. Instead, it was common for couples to confirm their pre-nuptial agreements through clandestine marriages. These were performed, without the publicity of banns, at irregular times and in irregular places like prison chapels and public houses, not only by laymen but also by impoverished clergy. For a fee, they would preside over vows which canon law in England still regarded as equivalent to a church marriage.

The worst of these rackets were the Fleet marriages, which Lord Hardwicke's Act did succeed in bringing to an end. These illicit and disreputable ceremonies had originated in Trinity Minories and

Duke's Place, St James's, London, whose ecclesiastical incumbents claimed immunity from the Bishop of London's jurisdiction. The practice had been adopted by clerical prisoners in the Fleet debtors' prison in 1616 and soon spread to rival marrying places — the Mayfair, the Mint and the Savoy. For a fee, anybody could be married to anybody, no questions asked, and so these marriage houses became a favourite destination of drunks and adventurers. In the streets outside, touts would drum up custom with the slogan 'Walk in and be married'. (Such weddings are the subject of *The Chaplain of the Fleet*, an 1881 novel by the great campaigner for social reform, Sir Walter Besant, and James Rice.)

Even the Marriage Act of 1823, which superseded Lord Hardwicke's Act, left open the question of informal marriages (which are still legally valid in Scotland). Only since the middle of the nineteenth century has it generally been agreed by English lawyers that all secular forms of marriage other than those allowed by statute are invalid.

Who Can You Marry and Who Can You Not?

In England, at least, the questions are fairly easy to answer. Marriage under sixteen years of age is forbidden. A person under eighteen must obtain consent to marry from both parents if they are living together, or, if they are separated or divorced, from the parent who has custody of the minor. If one parent is dead, the other's consent is necessary; if the deceased appointed a guardian, he or she must also consent. But if the person whose consent is required refuses to grant it, the court, on application, can overturn that decision and rule in favour of the proposed marriage. However, a Law Commission report published in July 1988 recommends ending the legal requirement of parental consent for the marriage of under-eighteens because, it says, it is 'illogical, easily circumvented or surmounted and of doubtful benefit to the very children it is trying to help.'

Such recommendations, which may form the framework for a government Bill, would, if implemented, bring English law into line with Scotland, where anyone over sixteen may marry without parental consent, and no residential qualification is required (hence the ease of circumvention referred to in the Law Commission report). Scottish marriages must be notified by both parties to the registrar of the district fifteen days before the marriage is to take place. At the end of this period, the registrar issues a marriage schedule which should be handed over to the minister at the ceremony.

If young lovers today decide to run off together to Scotland, this is the only way in which they can marry. They should abandon any thoughts they may have had about Gretna Green, which first sprang to prominence as a destination for eloping couples in 1754, as a direct consequence of Lord Hardwicke's Act the previous year. The last legally binding wedding over the blacksmith's anvil there took place in 1940, after which the Marriage (Scotland) Act 1939 made Scottish law more consonant with English. Prior to that, all that had been required for marriage north of the border was a declaration before witnesses, regardless of age or parental consent. Since then, elopers have been referred to nearby Gretna Register Office. A mock ceremony is still available at Gretna Green —

in 1985, 1,319 couples were 'married' there — but it's a tourist attraction only, and has no force in law.

The law governing consanguinity and affinity was set out in the Marriage Act 1949. It is now possible for a man to marry his:

Deceased wife's sister
Deceased brother's wife
Deceased wife's brother's daughter
Deceased wife's sister's daughter
Father's deceased brother's wife
Mother's deceased brother's wife
Deceased wife's father's sister
Deceased wife's mother's sister
Brother's deceased son's wife
Sister's deceased son's wife.

The same applies in reverse to women. However, a divorced spouse is prohibited from marrying his or her sister-in-law or brother-in-law.

In the Book of Common Prayer there is a Table of Kindred and Affinity, 'wherein whosoever are related are forbidden by the Church of England to marry together'. According to this Table, a man may not marry his:

Mother	Father's father's wife
Daughter	Mother's father's wife
Father's mother	Wife's father's mother
Mother's mother	Wife's mother's daughter
Son's daughter	Wife's son's daughter
Daughter's daughter	Wife's daughter's daughter
Sister	Son's son's wife
Father's daughter	Daughter's son's wife
Mother's daughter	Father's sister
Wife's mother	Mother's sister
Wife's daughter	Brother's daughter

Father's wife   Sister's daughter
Son's wife

A woman may not marry her:

Father	Father's mother's husband
Son	Mother's mother's husband
Father's father	Husband's father's father
Mother's father	Husband's mother's father
Son's son	Husband's son's son
Daughter's son	Husband's son's son
Brother	Husband's daughter's son
Father's son	Son's daughter's husband
Mother's son	Daughter's daughter's husband
Husband's father	Father's brother
Husband's son	Mother's brother
Mother's husband	Brother's son
Daughter's husband	Sister's son

Where and When Can You Marry?

Marriages should normally be conducted on reg
istered premises, ie, in a church or register office
(Exception is made in cases where one party is too il
to be moved and is not expected to recover.) This ma
change if new plans to deregulate the civil marriag
laws come into force. In a written reply in Decembe
1987, Lord Skelmersdale, then Under Secretary o
State at the Department of Health and Social Securit
(DHSS), outlined a government scheme to scrap th
residential qualification rules and thus allow couple
to marry anywhere in Britain. Historic houses an
council-owned castles could be offered to couples wil
ing to pay more than the standard licence fee for
civil ceremony. Local authorities would be at libert
to lay on extras like banquets and photographers, i

special wedding rooms. In the meantime, anyone with a desire to marry underwater on a coral reef must go to Mauritius. At Port Louis, two Danish tourists, Fleming Koch and Nina Tollgard, used diver's sign language to take their vows before a Mauritian civil servant watching from a glass-bottomed boat. The witness was a diving instructor.

Before a Church of England wedding can take place, the banns of matrimony must, by law, be called in the parish or parishes in which the parties reside. If they are to be married in a third church, the banns must be published there also. In such cases, the couple must either take up residence in the parish where they are to be married fifteen days before the wedding, or else be put on the electoral roll of the church and attend services there for six months before the wedding.

When calling the banns, the clergyman must read aloud during Morning or Evening Service the form of words prescribed in the Book of Common Prayer:

'I publish the Banns of Marriage between *N.* of — and *N.* of —. If any of you know cause, or just impediment, why these two persons should not be joined together in holy Matrimony, ye are to declare it. This is the first/second/third time of asking.'

This must be recited on three Sundays (not necessarily three consecutive Sundays) preceding the marriage ceremony. If three months elapse between the time of publication and the marriage, the banns become void and the parties must obtain a licence or agree

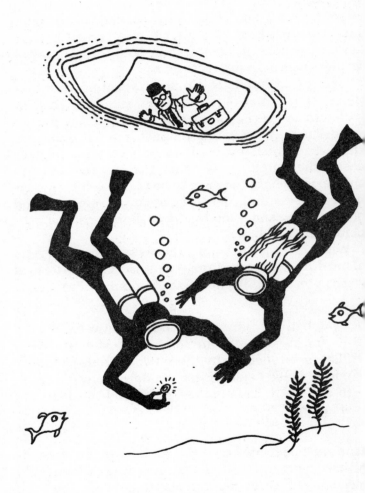

Getting down to it

to a republication of the banns. The purpose of the banns is, as everyone supposes, to flush out bigamists.

If for any reason, like pressure of time or desire for privacy, the banns cannot be called in the normal way, a common licence must be obtained. This is done by application to the Diocesan Registrar, or any surrogate, for granting marriage licences in the relevant diocese (*see* Useful Addresses). This enables the marriage to be solemnised in a licensed church or chapel. In cases where the parties wish to be married in a church outside the parishes in which they habitually reside, and they cannot meet the requirements set out above, it is necessary to obtain a special licence from the Archbishop of Canterbury. Although this is not difficult to obtain, it remains a privilege, not a right (*see* Useful Addresses).

Marriages may be solemnised at any time between 8 am and 6 pm on any day of the year, even Christmas Day, Good Friday and Easter Sunday. The officiating clergyman must ensure that there are at least two witnesses present, and that the entries in the registry book are witnessed by two people. One of these is often the Best Man, the other the Bride's father.

In a register office, the marriage must take place in the presence of the Registrar of Marriages and the Superintendent Registrar. Notice of the marriage must be entered in the Superintendent Registrar's notice book (usually displayed in a Town Hall) twenty-one days before the issue of the licence during which time objections can be raised. The marriage may then take place at any time within three months of the day on which the notice was

entered. Here again, the Bride's father and the Best
Man frequently witness the signatures of the Bride
and Groom. Incidentally, it is interesting to note that
when Lord Skelmersdale was making preliminary
enquiries into the feasibility of the DHSS proposals
he interviewed fifty Superintendent Registrars and
only one of them had ever heard of a notice thus
displayed leading to a valid objection to a marriage,
and that was purely by chance.

Some American Marriage Laws

In the United States, marriage is now universally
on the civil contract basis, but religious ceremonies
are authorised in all states provided that a marriage
licence has been obtained. Yet the laws of marriage
differ from state to state, sometimes remarkably.
For example:

- California has no minimum age for marriage with
  parental consent.

- Delaware and Georgia will waive the legal minimum age if the woman is pregnant.

- Some states require certificates of immunity from
  contagious syphilis or gonorrhoea or both. These
  are California, Idaho, Indiana, Montana, Missis-
  sippi, New Jersey, North Carolina, Pennsylvania,
  Utah and West Virginia.

- In California, Idaho, Indiana, Montana, Nebras-
  ka and Wyoming, women require a certificate of
  immunity from rubella (German measles) unless
  they are over a certain age or certified sterile.

- Colorado and Illinois require proof of freedom from

sickle cell anaemia, while New York may require it if deemed necessary.

- Several states require a more general medical examination. Although its object is not explicitly to detect venereal infection, Hawaii's state law leaves little doubt what is being alluded to when it insists that 'neither party be afflicted with any loathsome disease concealed from, and unknown to, other party.' Other states in this category are Florida, Massachusetts, New Jersey, New Mexico, Tennessee, Vermont, Washington, Wisconsin.

- In New Hampshire there is no examination, but a marriage is voidable if one party is subsequently found to have had gonorrhoea or syphilis on the wedding day.

- Arizona, Arkansas and New York used to have obligatory medical tests but have now abolished them.

- New Jersey will not grant a marriage licence if either party is under the influence of drink or drugs.

- Hawaii forbids marriage between those with any blood tie at all.

- The lowest legal age for marriage in the USA is in Kansas and Massachusetts. There, it is fourteen for males and twelve for females.

- Some states specify that the couple should be of opposite sexes.

- In North Dakota, a person of standing in the

Neither party is an habitual criminal

community must swear an affidavit that neithe
party is an habitual criminal.

Marriage and Customs in Other Countries

Even bearing in mind the eccentricities of the abov
there is throughout the western world a remarkabl
homogeneity in the concept and execution of mar
riage, whether it be marriage by civil or religiou
ceremony or, as in France, by both. Although cano
law turned a terminable civil contract into a mysti
and sacramental union of souls and bodies which
regarded as indivisible until death, many present da
appurtenances of marriage are considerably olde
than Christianity. Rice and confetti, for exampl

are pagan symbols of fecundity, and when clergymen insist that they be thrown outside the precincts of the church, one may wonder whether their sole concern is for the mess that will thereby be created.

Between this and the custom and practice in non-western societies, the contrast could hardly be greater. Although there are laws prohibiting marriage between certain close kin, these are socially rather than biologically determined, and a certain amount of genetic inbreeding may occur. There are few instances of marriage between mother and son and father and daughter, but there have been legitimate marriages between brother and sister in the Marshall Islands and Hawaii, as well as in ancient Egyptian, Incan and Irish royal families.

Not all societies demand sexual exclusivity: among the Nayar of southern India, marriage lasts only three days, whereupon the wife is free to have sex with other men. Some civilisations blink at infidelity on condition that children from the extra-marital union are affiliated to the legitimate husband's kin. The strictness of the rules of marriage are to a large extent predicated by the number of rights transferred on marriage. The more one partner hands over to the other — sexual services, domestic labour, rights over children, protection from enemies, payment of taxes and the like — the greater the penalties for transgression. In England, the increased ease of divorce derives in part from the modern woman's greater financial independence.

In some societies, notably in East Africa, marriage is not dissolved upon the death of one partner: a man who dies without issue has his wife married to his name by his brother. She bears children by the brother, and their children are legally those of the deceased man whose heirs then inherit his wealth and sacrifice to his spirit. This is called Ghost Marriage. Leviration, a similar custom, was practised by the ancient Hebrews in accordance with Deuteronomy 25, *v–x* and survives today in some African peoples. The same process in reverse, called sororate, was adopted by North American Indians of the Great Basin.

The study of marriage in various societies casts fascinating light upon the social and religious milieux of the people who use them. The purpose of referring to them here is to demonstrate that in God's house there are many mansions, and that there are more things in heaven and earth than are dreamed of in the philosophy of even the most portentous clergyman or registrar. Such thoughts may help those who will shortly have to make a speech themselves to resist being overwhelmed by the pomp of the marriage ceremony.

II

AN ENGAGEMENT IS ANNOUNCED

A man and a woman have decided to marry. The first thing they should do is announce the fact to interested parties. This is usually done in one or more of the following ways.

First, by a notice in the 'Forthcoming Marriages' column of a national or local newspaper. This is a case where tradition may be said to outweigh practicality: does everyone you wish to inform take the paper in which you have chosen to advertise? Do they all look at the Court and Social page? In Great Britain, it has long been fashionable to use *The Times* for this purpose: the 1960s advertising slogan 'The Top People's Newspaper' retains its resonance, even today; but others may prefer *The Guardian* or *The Independent*. More locally-oriented people (and by this is meant people whose circle of friends and relatives is largely confined within a small and tightly-knit community) may prefer their local rag. The usual form of words in the announcement is this:

> 'The engagement is announced between Alistair, son of Mr and Mrs Octavian Losasso, of Tewkesbury, Gloucestershire, and Agnes, daughter of Mr and Mrs Barnaby Truslove, of Moreton-in-Marsh, Worcestershire'

The Times will not allow advertisements phrased in

any other way, unless there is to be no engagement as such, in which case the wording 'the marriage will take place . . .' is acceptable. 'Son' and 'daughter' may be qualified as necessary with 'only', 'elder', 'eldest', 'younger' or 'youngest'. The only variants are in cases of one or both parents' death (' . . .daughter of the late Mr Barnaby Truslove and of Mrs Annabel Truslove . . .'); divorce (' . . .daughter of Mr Barnaby Truslove and of Mrs Annabel Truslove . . .'), and remarriage (' . . .daughter of Mr Barnaby Truslove and of Mrs William Collins . . .'). Obviously, if a parent's change of surname gives rise to ambiguity about the child's surname, then the child's surname should be stated.

The other ways of announcing an engagement are by throwing a party and by word of mouth. Both ensure reaching more of the right people (ie, those who you want to tell), but neither has the stylishness (to say nothing of the cachet and the snob-appeal) of a newspaper advertisement. These methods are not mutually exclusive; nor is any one of them obligatory: you can always marry today and announce the fact to your family and friends tomorrow. Indeed, in one recent case, the marriage came as something of a shock to the Bride. Heather Barden thought she was going to spend lunchtime celebrating her qualification as a staff nurse. Instead, a friend tricked her into going to a register office where her boyfriend Philip Richardson, was waiting with thirty guests. He proposed to her on the threshold and ten minutes later they were married.

An engagement party (as distinct from a party at which an engagement is announced) is usually for only a few relatives and intimate friends, and is not infrequently the occasion of the first meeting of the Bride's parents and the Groom's. The only point of etiquette at an engagement party is that the Bride's father may propose a toast to the couple, and the Groom may reply, thanking everyone for their good wishes and proposing a toast to both sets of parents.

The announcement of the engagement is usually taken care of by the Bride's family, and it is upon them that most of the other early duties fall: the time, date and place of the wedding and the reception, deciding the number to be invited, the compilation of the wedding guest list and the sending out of invitations are all arranged by them. An exception to this general rule was the marriage of Julie Dixon and Alan Perkins. The groom, a London milkman, handed out invitations to all 1,036 customers on his delivery round; he received over five hundred acceptances. He said that he wasn't worried about the expense, he just wanted as many friends as possible to be a part of his big day. 'I'll make sure they all get a drink afterwards', he promised. 'And it won't be milk', he added significantly. One customer responded to this generosity by offering the new Mr and Mrs Perkins the keys to his Spanish villa for a free two-week honeymoon: cast thy bread upon the waters . . .

Choosing a Best Man and the Attendants

At this point in the proceedings the Groom should turn his mind towards the appointment of his Best Man. It is easy to compose a list a qualities for him to look for when he comes to make his choice, but its usefulness is questionable. If he intends to make the appointment from among his old friends, it is reasonable to assume that he will already know

Best men: some not to choose

enough about their characters and therefore naturally eliminate from his consideration anyone who is as punctual as the White Rabbit, as tactful as an investigative journalist, as sober as Falstaff, or as succinct an orator as the Ancient Mariner. It used to be held that the Best Man should be unmarried, but this rather pointless custom has now fallen into disuse and may safely be ignored.

You can, if you wish, have two Best Men. Peter Sellers did it when he married Britt Ekland in 1964. They were actors David Lodge and Graham Stark. Jon Cedermark of Lancashire used a six foot tailor's mannequin called Ken, but the registrar at his wedding would not allow him to be brought into the service. Royal Grooms tend to have a supporter rather than a Best Man (Prince Charles, for example, had Prince Andrew), but this is only a nominal distinction: the role is exactly the same. There is nothing to prevent a woman from being a Best Man.

Contrary to popular belief, it is not a good idea for the Best Man to be an obsessive pre-planner. If he or anyone else involved in the wedding wishes to time the journey from the church to the reception, so be it. Any number of rehearsals and dummy runs will not forestall road works or demonstrations or overturned dustcarts which will, if they see fit, conspire to make you late. By the same token, no amount of care will ensure that everyone has transport from the ceremony to the reception. If, on the day, someone is without a seat in a car, he will almost certainly tell the Best Man of his predicament, and a solution will have to be found there and then. Excessive preparation may help to fill up time in the nervous months preceding the wedding, but worry beads are just as much good. You are, after all, planning a Bacchanalia with knobs on, not the Normandy Landings. If the Best Man must be anything, he must be one who can improvise, think on his feet, cross each bridge when he comes to it, take each game as it comes and any of the other clichés associated with football management. During the early stages of preparation, all the Best Man has to do is take an intelligent interest in the details of date, time, place, etc, and generally be supportive to the Groom. The Groom, for his part, will no doubt welcome a male confidant during all the ensuing — predominantly female — activity.

Once the choice of Best Man is made and the candidate has accepted, it is important for the Groom to introduce him to the chief bridesmaid. This may be done at a dinner held by the engaged couple. As the wedding day draws near, it will be necessary for the two main attendants to liaise quite closely over each other's arrangements, so the better they know each other and the better they get get on, the more smoothly the wedding may be expected to run.

Bridesmaids and pages are appointed by the Bride, and tend to be her brothers and sisters or nephews and nieces. Elaine Alexander, from Birmingham, picked her pet Alsatian Tara as bridesmaid and her springer spaniel Monty as page boy. Tara wore a pink and white carnation necktie, while Monty turned out in a maroon suit and velvet bow tie. Birmingham Register Office refused to let the dogs into the ceremony.

The Groom's next responsibility is the choice of Ushers. These tend to be Groom's close friends and/or the brothers of the bride. Their duties are not strictly defined, but it is usual to find them performing the following necessary functions on the wedding day:

Usher 1: hand out service sheets to the congregation at the church door. (He may also be first reserve if the Best Man is indisposed, incapacitated or struck dumb with terror at the prospect of public speaking.)

Usher 2: stand at the foot of the aisle and ask each guest 'Bride or Groom?', meaning whose friend or relative are they. According to their reply, they will be shown to a seat either on the left of the church (Bride) or the right (Groom). Holders of this office should be warned that there will inevitably be those who answer 'Both'. In such case, ask more questions if there is time; if not, or if there is felt to be a significant risk of hearing the guest's detailed reminiscences of three decades' intimacy with one or other of the happy couple, direct them to the side which has fewer people.

Both Usher 1 and Usher 2 should try to keep the back rows of the church free for latecomers; they might also suggest aisle seats for guests with young children, so that they may leave unobtrusively if the children get restless during the service.

Usher 3: stand halfway down the aisle to seat the guests. (Not, you may rightly assume, a vital function, but a convenient job to give to someone you feel needs something to do.)

Usher 4: stand at the church door and escort the Bride's mother to her seat on arrival. (This may be incorporated into the job of Usher 1; alternatively, Usher 4 may also help Usher 1 hand out service sheets.)

Usher 5: organise the parking of cars outside.

On the subject of cars, it is never too early to think about the principal characters' transport to and from the wedding. It will be helpful to consider that separate vehicles will be needed for the following parties:

A *Before the Wedding*
    1 The Bride's mother and attendants
    2 The Bride and the Bride's father
B *After the Wedding*
    1 The Bride and Groom
    2 Attendants
    3 The Bride's parents

Several companies hire out unusual forms of transport: you can get a New York taxi or a pre-war motorbike; in the horse-drawn line, there are broughams, landaus, phaetons, even a glass coach with four grey horses. A Stoke-on-Trent hire company has available for weddings the white 'Popemobile' used by John Paul II on his visit to Great Britain in 1982. Interested parties should, however, bear in mind that this vehicle is one of a kind, and that the other principals may feel slighted by having to travel in a run-of-the-mill Rolls Royce.

Wedding Invitations

These are normally sent out six weeks before the wedding. Their layout is entirely up to the Bride's

The Popemobile

family: nothing is *de rigueur*, no design can be *de trop*. However, invitations are usually engraved on a piece of card folded in half, inside which is the following form of words:

Mr and Mrs Barnaby Truslove
request the pleasure of
your company at the marriage
of their daughter
Agnes
to
Mr Alistair Losasso
at St Olaf's Church, Mayfair
on Saturday, 29 July 1989
at 2.30 pm
and afterwards at
Claridge's

RSVP
Headlong Hall
Moreton-in-Marsh, Worcestershire

This is where the host and hostess are the father and mother of the bride. Variants are as follows:

A If the Bride's mother is the sole hostess:
Mrs Barnaby Truslove
requests the pleasure, etc . . .

B If the Bride's mother is a widow and the sole hostess:
Mrs Annabel Truslove
requests the pleasure, etc . . .

C If the Bride's father is the sole host:
Mr Barnaby Truslove
requests the pleasure, etc . . .

D   If the Bride's mother and stepfather are hostess and host

> Mr and Mrs William Collins
> request the pleasure of
> your company at the marriage
> of her daughter Agnes Truslove, etc . . .

E If the Bride's father and stepmother are host and hostess:

> Mr and Mrs Barnaby Truslove
> request the pleasure of
> your company at the marriage
> of his daughter, etc . . .

F If the Bride's stepmother is the sole hostess:

> Mrs Barnaby Truslove
> requests the pleasure of
> your company at the marriage
> of her step-daughter, etc . . .

G If the Bride's parents, though divorced, are joint host and hostess:

> Mr Barnaby Truslove
> and
> Mrs William Collins
> request the pleasure of
> your company at the marriage
> of their daughter, etc . . .

H If the Bride's parents, though divorced, are joint host and hostess, but the wife has not remarried:

> Mr Barnaby Truslove
> and
> Mrs Barnaby Truslove
> request the pleasure, etc . . .

In cases where the Bride's relatives, guardians or godparents are host and hostess, the form is the same, except that the Bride's surname should be included where it differs from theirs. If the Bride herself is the hostess, the form is:

> Miss Agnes Truslove
> requests the pleasure of
> your company at her marriage to
> Mr Alistair Losasso . . .

'Honour' can be used instead of 'pleasure'. Note that in all cases the name of the guest should be written by hand in the top left hand corner of the invitation. The addition of 'and escort' or 'and partner' will allow guests to bring an unspecified companion with them. ('And friend' should be avoided, on the grounds that this would exclude a member of the guest's family.)

If the church/register office is too small to accommodate all the guests, invitations should read 'at the Reception to be held after the marriage of . . .'. In this case, it is good form to place a note inside explaining why there is no invitation to the ceremony itself. *Never* is a guest invited to the ceremony but not to the reception.

If the wedding is to be postponed because of a family bereavement, a card should be sent out with the following wording:

> 'Owing to the recent death of Mr Barnaby Truslove,
> Mrs Truslove deeply regrets that she is obliged
> to cancel the invitations to the marriage of
> their daughter Agnes to Mr Alistair Losasso.'

These should be engraved if time allows, but obviously in such extreme circumstances a handwritten note will suffice. It is understood that invitations will be sent out again when a new date is fixed. If it is decided notwithstanding a death in the family that the wedding will still take place, but quietly, the note should read:

'Owing to the recent death of her husband,
Mrs Barnaby Truslove regrets that she is obliged
to cancel the invitations to the marriage of
her daughter Agnes to Mr Alistair Losasso,
which will now take place very quietly on
Monday 21 August 1989.'

Invitations will then be sent out only to very close family and friends.

In the case of a postponement, the form is:

'Mr and Mrs Barnaby Truslove regret to announce
that, owing to the illness of Mr Truslove,
they are obliged to postpone the marriage of
their daughter Agnes to Mr Alistair Losasso
from Saturday 29 July 1989
to Monday 21 August 1989.'

In the unhappy event of a broken engagement, the following should be sent:

'Mr and Mrs Barnaby Truslove announce that
the marriage of their daughter Agnes to
Mr Alistair Losasso will not now take place.'

Replies to wedding invitations should bear the sender's address at the head of the page, and be in the third person:

Palace Terrace
London W8

Mr and Mrs Oliver Varney thank
Mr and Mrs Truslove for their kind invitation
for 29 July 1989,
which they accept with much pleasure
(*or*, which they have the honour to accept).

Or alternatively:

Palace Terrace
London W8

Mr and Mrs Oliver Varney thank
Mr and Mrs Truslove for their kind invitation
which they much regret being unable to accept.

(A reason may be given, eg, owing to
absence abroad.)

If a particular form of dress is to be prescribed for all guests, it should be indicated at the bottom of the invitation.

Dress

Very often, morning suits may be worn by the main characters — Groom, Best Man, Bride's father, Groom's father, Ushers — and by no one else. Black or grey shoes should be worn with such an outfit, never brown. Top hats traditionally accompany morning dress, but let those who intend to wear them be warned: indoors they must be carried; in cars they cannot be worn because there is insufficient headroom; they are invariably mixed up with other people's in piles in cloakrooms and end up being returned to the wrong costumier. That said, it would be most unusual to have morning dress without top hats and less fun too. For women at Church of England and Roman Catholic ceremonies, it is only customary for hats to be worn not, as is sometimes thought, compulsory for the head to be covered (*cf* synagogues, where men and women alike must cover their heads in the sight of God).

In general, there are no rules in the matter of dress at weddings, only customs. And if rules were made to be broken, what chance does poor tradition stand? None, in the case of Anita Calverley, who turned up to her church wedding dressed as if for a funeral: she wore something old, something new, something borrowed and everything in black. Her bridesmaids wore red ballet-length dresses. Significantly, the Reverend Eric Gunn, the clergyman who married her, had no objection whatever. 'I've married people in all hues and colours', he said. 'I can't remember seeing black before, but I really don't mind what anyone wears at a wedding.'

It is a nice, but by no means obligatory, touch for the Groom's accessories and those of his men to be the same — eg, silk ties or cravats of a particular colour; buttonholes dyed in the same way. One bizarre variation of this theme of matching accessories occurred at the wedding of Rosemary O'Boyle, assistant stage manager at The Queen's Theatre, London, which was then showing Brecht's *The Resistible Rise of Arturo Ui*. Eighteen members of the cast, led by Griff Rhys Jones, arrived at the church carrying cauliflowers (an abundance of which are thrown during a particularly riotous episode of the play). They held these aloft in a 'caulifloral' arch for Miss O'Boyle and her Groom Mr Mark Kancary, himself carrying a cauli, to pass under as they left the church.

The only rule in the matter of dress is that the Groom should provide and pay for the buttonholes (or Brassicae) of the Best Man and Ushers. At a civil wedding, the same rules apply: dress to conform with the wishes of the Bride's family, if specified; otherwise come as you wish, even come as you are. It is certain that registrars marry people wearing overalls as often as they marry them in tails.

The Wedding List

There are three methods of dealing with wedding presents. One is for the couple to go to a department store which offers the service known as 'The Bride's Book'. There, with the help of an assistant, they compile a list of the goods they need/hope to receive. The shop then keeps the master copy of the inventory while the Bride circulates copies among those of the guests who have asked to receive them. The guests telephone or visit the shop, make their choice and pay the bill. The item is then crossed off the list and sent to the home of the Bride's parents. This avoids duplication of presents.

The second method is to circulate a wedding list with no particular shop in mind. The guests should then ring the Bride and tell her which item they propose to buy. She will then delete it from the

A dozen pop-up toasters

list herself, and the guests will be left to make the purchase from a shop of their own choice.

The third method is to have no list at all, and leave the choice entirely to the guests. Couples who adopt this method often object to a conventional wedding list on the grounds either that 'we'd prefer them to buy us something personal, without any prompting', or that 'it seems too much like overt soliciting'.

To the first objection, the answer is that without a list you run the risk of returning from the honeymoon to a dozen pop-up toasters. To the second, the answer is more complicated. It is implicit in a wedding invitation that a party is being held at considerable expense in the expectation of a return on the investment in the form of presents. The British are perhaps reticent to a fault about these financial realities. Compare the practice at a Greek Cypriot wedding. There, no presents are expected, but during the service members of the Groom's family pass among the congregation and offer buttonholes to the male guests. Anyone who takes one becomes the Groom's *koumbaros* (which loosely translates as something between 'Best Man' and 'sponsor'), of which there can be any number. The *koumbari* then participate in the protracted Greek Orthodox ceremonial exchange of rings. Later, at the reception, they are picked out by the family and they must then use a pin to stick money onto the Groom's clothing as he dances with his Bride. This is a refreshingly candid approach to what is, in reality, a business transaction: a wedding really is no different from a bottle party, and there are names for people who turn up at those without any wine.

'Shower parties' are an interesting American custom: a party is held to which the guests bring some gift for the marital home. For example, at a bedroom shower, everyone would be expected to bring sheets, pillowcases, towels and the like; at a kitchen shower, cutlery, crockery and glassware. In North Dakota, some couples go even further and raise money by holding an auction at the reception: the highest bidder is permitted to remove and keep the Bride's garter!

These are early days for the Best Man; the pace will hot up nearer the event. But for the time being, that is all ye know, and all ye need to know.

III
THE STAG NIGHT AND ELEVENTH HOUR

There is no reason why the Stag Party should take place on the eve of the wedding; indeed, there are many good reasons why it should not. The wedding day calls for a clear head — there's work to be done, much to be remembered; a hangover is not the best aide-mémoire. The idea of the Stag Night is that a group of men should get together for the purpose of eating and drinking to excess to celebrate the Groom's last night of freedom and is customarily organised by the Best Man. Whether or not it is the Groom's last night of freedom depends to a large extent upon the choice of Bride, but however that may be, the occasion is taken as an opportunity for the Groom to talk at length and leisure to old friends whom he may not get a chance to see more than fleetingly at the wedding itself.

In some cases, the total cost of the evening may be borne by the Groom; but it is now more usual for the guests to pay for themselves, and to split the Groom's contribution between them. The Best Man may wish to divide the bill when it arrives and pass the hat round there and then, or alternatively to pay for the whole lot himself and undertake to advise the guests of the price per head by post later.

Unless you are simply going out for a night in

the pub, it is important to book the entertainment in advance, and therefore to be sure of the number of people attending. Be warned that some restaurants, once bitten by the exuberance of a Stag Night party, may be twice shy of accepting further similar bookings: it may be necessary to shop around before finding a willing taker.

What is even more important, if the Groom has to get home by car, is that the Best Man should remain sober to do the driving. The Best Man should pick up the Groom at the start of the evening and be his minder until he has been safely deposited in his home at the end of it. (Note 'in his home'. Outside it or near it will not do: he must not end his 'last night of freedom' slumped on the front doorstep between the milk bottles and the rubbish bin.) The Best Man will do well to remind himself at the start of the evening just how many such events end in disaster. A year does not pass without several newspaper stories of Grooms who have been seriously injured or killed as a result of being drunk without proper supervision: they fall off walls, drown in the bath, even get themselves shot in the leg. In one recent case reported in a Sunday newspaper, although the Groom got through the evening unscathed, the Best Man was arrested after getting into a punch-up with thirty people. They were all charged with affray, and magistrates at Oswestry, Shropshire only granted the Best Man bail to attend the wedding on condition that he didn't drink.

The Best Man may consider that it behoves him to make a speech on the Stag Night. He may alternatively take the wiser course of saving himself for the wedding day oration. If the Best Man is a seasoned and proficient public speaker, he should beware the dangers of stealing the Groom's thunder — it is after all his show, not the Best Man's, and one of the greatest compliments an attendant lord can pay to his liege is not to upstage him. If, however, the Best Man is becomingly nervous about his impending speech, he should not make the mistake of thinking of the Stag Night as an opportunity to polish his finest *mots*. Even the best jokes are only funny once, and a wisecrack that will evoke raucous guffaws from a gang of rugby players in their cups will most likely be greeted with silence when it is repeated at the reception. By then, the only people who will not have heard it are the prim lot from the distaff side, and they are not renowned for filling the auditorium with laughter. Let the watchword be the inscription on the self-portrait of Salvator Rosa: *Aut tace aut loquere meliora silentio*, 'either keep quiet or say something better than silence'.

Now a word about the Stag Night indiscretion. It is a commonly held notion that on the Stag Night the Groom will wish or is supposed to engage in some form of sexual dalliance with a woman other than his betrothed. The idea probably dates from an age when men generally approached their nuptials without any previous sexual experience. The professional services of a certain type of woman were therefore sought in order to give the Groom his initiation into the arts at which he needed to be proficient by his wedding night. The legacy of this is that 'the lads' often spend the greater part of the evening talking about the prospect of getting the Groom laid. They would be well advised to forget all about it. Men who are about to be married tend to be serious about their intentions;

44

AVT TACE
AVT LOQVERE MELIORA
SILENTIO.

Salvator Rosa (1615–1673)

even if they are not, it would be reckless of them to contemplate such a liaison in front of a coterie of rib-digging witnesses. The myth still has credence in some quarters — at one Stag Party held in a famous low-life establishment in London's West End, after the Best Man had paid a bill for food and copious drink for twelve people which came to nearly five hundred pounds, one of the hostesses asked whether,

45

'bearing in mind that this is a Stag Night and that', there would be any 'extra services' required. After perfunctory consultation with the Groom, the Best Man in question was able to decline on his behalf with stiff formality. There would have been more chance of wheedling an indiscretion out of Sir Galahad.

Last, it is necessary to say something about Hen Nights (why Hen should in this context be the feminine of Stag is a mystery). It seems that the tradition grew up as a feminist riposte to the Stag Night. It usually takes the form of a meal in a restaurant, at which a great deal of gossip is traded. Sometimes the clutch of Hens will arrange for the Bride to receive a singing telegram or a visit from a male stripper.

Wheedling an indiscretion out of Sir Galahad

Over their contribution to the revels it is better to draw a veil of discretion and move on quickly to a more edifying subject.

The Best Man's Last Minute Duties

The days immediately preceding the wedding will naturally be busy but should not be hectic or fraught. The Best Man's contribution should be aimed at bringing a note of calm into the proceedings. A checklist is provided at the end of this book for the Groom and Best Man to run through during the last week. It is important to remember that it is not the job of either man to do all these things, merely to make sure either that they are going to be done by someone, or that they do not need to be done at all.

The wedding ring is, of course, something that will have been purchased by the Groom in consultation with the Bride. All the Best Man has to do is take it from the Groom on the wedding morning and make sure he doesn't lose it. Many people also take along a curtain ring in case of emergency, but presumably most of us can be relied upon not to lose credit cards and cheque book, so why should we doubt our ability to keep hold of a band of metal? Yes, there is a possibility that you will drop it down the grille in the floor of the church, but if you look at it rationally, you have to concede that the danger is more imagined than real.

It may be that the Groom wants himself, Best Man and Ushers dressed identically in clothing hired from the same outfitter, in which case it will be necessary to arrange a date for the group fitting. What may be more practical than organising a meeting of as many as nine people (Groom, Best Man, Bride's father, Groom's father, five Ushers) during weekday working hours is to leave the Ushers and male parents to their own devices, relying on their intelligence and taste, and just get a simultaneous fitting for the Groom and Best Man.

If the Groom is going to the ceremony in the Best Man's car, another car or taxi should be laid on for the couple's going away. Few things are more embarrassing than the spectacle of the Best Man driving the happy couple away to the wedding night hotel, looking for all the world as if he may be about to exercise *droit de seigneur*.

A church minister may request an informal rehearsal for all the principals in the wedding ceremony. This will be held in the church a few days before the event. Here is an excellent opportunity to put your minds at rest and for the minister to outline any particular bugbear he may have. He may, for example, wish for cameras and tape recorders not to be used during the service; he may wish to adumbrate his objections to the throwing of confetti in the churchyard.

It is on the wedding day that the Best Man really comes into his own. He must be responsible for waking the Groom (by telephone, by personal visit, or by staying with him the night before), and for helping him to dress. This latter need not be interpreted too literally: checking to see that ties/cravats and button-holes are on straight will usually suffice. An assiduous Best Man may even iron the Groom's shirt, but this may be regarded as devotion above and beyond the call of duty.

Likewise, the definitive Best Man may wish to enquire of the Bride's family whether there is anything he can do to help them. Yet he would act

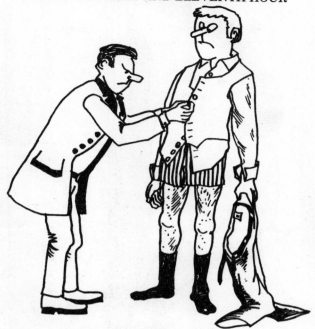

Helping the Groom to dress

more prudently if he put them as far out of mind as possible: there is a tendency in human nature to find a job for those who offer their services, regardless of its importance. Don't end up nipping out to find safety pins or extra paper napkins: your Groom needs you more than they do. All the Best Man needs to contact the Bride's family for is to ensure that any Telemessages (telegrams) sent to the Bride's family home are brought to the ceremony and handed over to him in time for the reception.

It is for the Best Man to make sure that he and the Groom have all the documents and props they will need: the ring, the banns certificate (if the

Parachuting to the church on time

marriage is taking place in a diocese other than that in which the Groom normally resides), clothes for going away in, money. For the honeymoon, the Groom should have passport and tickets. Get the Groom to the church early, the earlier the better. Take time to soak up the atmosphere, like a team strolling on the Wembley pitch before the Cup Final. Such calm before the storm will help both men to remember any last-minute omissions, and leave time for them to be rectified. All you will then need to do is make sure that the Ushers have the service sheets and pay the fees to the minister. After that, go for a last drink in the nearest pub, or do something similar to calm the nerves: a frame of snooker might not be a bad idea. When Steve Francis married Kay Shatford in 1988, he and his Best Man passed the time before the ceremony by parachuting to the church from three thousand feet up: *chacun à son gout.*

IV
THE CEREMONY

In a Church

Now they've got this far, all the Groom and Best Man have to do is stand at the top of the aisle at the front of the right hand pew and await the arrival of the guests and Bride.

When she comes, one of two things will happen. Either she and her father will proceed up the aisle and meet the minister and Groom at the altar, or she will be met by the minister at the porch. In this case, the chief chorister bearing the cross will lead the way up the aisle, followed by the choir, the minister, the Bride wearing her veil (if she has one: she is under no obligation to do so), and on her father's right arm, and then the bridal attendants in order of seniority. In either case, immediately upon the Bride's arrival all but one of the Ushers should move to their seats to make room for the procession, one remaining to escort the Bride's mother to her seat on the left of the altar. The Bride may enter during the first hymn, but more usually she is accompanied by a piece of music of her own choice. Of course the best known and most popular of these is the Bridal March from Wagner's *Lohengrin*, but the choice is almost limitless. One might for example favour Elgar's *Imperial March* or *Pomp and Circumstance* No 4, Walton's *Crown Imperial*, the 'Hornpipe in D' from Handel's *Water Music*, 'The Grand March of the Druids' from Bellini's *Norma*, or the 'Grand March' from Verdi's *Aida*. The rule is, you can have whatever you like as long as the clergyman agrees to it and it isn't sacrilegious. (*Sympathy for the Devil* by the Rolling Stones, for example, is most unlikely to satisfy either criterion).

As the first chords are played, the congregation rises and the Groom and Best Man move from their seats to the right of the chancel steps. This is the moment for the Best Man to hand the ring discreetly to the Groom. A good Best Man will not think that he is somehow failing in his duty if he omits to perform an elaborate mime to indicate to the assembly that he has mislaid it. Such hamming is obtrusive and cringe-making. Someone (usually the chief bridesmaid) should take the Bride's bouquet so that her hands are free for the ring. If no one is available for this task, a hassock may be placed within convenient reach. If the Bride is to give a ring to the Groom, she may call upon either her father or the chief bridesmaid to hold it for her until it is required at the ceremony.

The order of service will vary slightly according to the wishes of the individual minister, but each service will incorporate entrance music, two or three hymns, the marriage itself, an address, prayers, the signing of the register, a blessing and recession music. (The Marriage Service from the Book of Common Prayer is reproduced in full in the next Chapter). The usual duration of the service is approximately thirty minutes. At some point in the proceedings the minister will lead the Bride, Groom, Best Man and bridal party into the vestry for the signing of the register. Someone should remember to bring the Bride's bouquet: if no one else does, the Best Man should not fail.

Once installed in the vestry, the atmosphere momentarily becomes less formal; there is much kissing, handshaking and congratulations. It is as well to keep all this as brief as possible: there is likely to be another couple marrying later in the day, and it is unfair to make them wait unnecessarily.

The Bride and Groom sign the register; the Bride signs first, using her maiden name. When both parties have signed, the minister will ask for two witnesses. Anyone present over the age of eighteen may sign, but it is usually the Best Man, the chief bridesmaid, or the mother or father of the Bride or Groom who are called upon to do so. Photographs are permitted in the vestry.

After that, the Bride and Groom (Groom on the right, leaving his sword hand free) lead the recession down the aisle and out of the church. The Best Man and the bridal party follow the couple, the bellringers chime forth the glad tidings and the organist plays a triumphal march. The most popular choice of recession music is Mendelssohn's *A Midsummer Night's Dream* (Opus 61 No 9), but among other possibilities are Purcell's *Trumpet Voluntary*, the 'Minuet' from *Berenice* by Handel and Guilmant's *Spring Song*.

Payments are nowadays usually made in advance, but if they have not been made it is the Best Man's duty to hand over the marriage fees, the clergyman's fee, the organist's fee, the bellringers' fee, the choir's fee and something for the verger, to whom the money should be given in a sealed envelope. Then, unless it is raining (in which case the whole operation may be carried over to the reception), the official photographer will be let loose among the guests. The Best Man should try to shepherd those required for the large group family photographs into the right place, and help the cameraman to get the small people to the front.

Bride and Groom should leave for the reception first, escorted to their car by the Best Man. Bridesmaids leave next, then the Bride's parents. The Best Man will probably get people asking about transport to the reception, but he should slip away as soon as possible himself: at the reception he will be more useful, and he will need as much time as possible to accustom himself to the surroundings and prepare himself spiritually for the most harrowing part of his duty: the speech.

In a Register Office

Marriage in a register office is the same thing without the ceremonial embellishments. The Best Man should hand over the ring to the Groom unobtrusively at an appropriate moment, although strictly there is no necessity for a ring to play any part in a civil wedding. Bride and Groom arrive at the office together and in the presence of at least two witnesses, apart from the Registrar and the Superintendent Registrar, they say aloud the following:

'I do solemnly declare that
I know not of any lawful
impediment why I, *N*. should
not be joined together in
marriage to *N*.'

Afterwards, each should say:

'I call upon these persons
here present to witness that

I, *N*. do take thee, *N*., for
my lawful wedded husband/wife'.

The register is then signed by the Bride and Groom,
two witnesses and the two Registrars in front of the
assembly.

Weddings in Other Circumstances

If the Bride is a widow, the church wedding takes
much the same form as above, except that it is traditional, though not obligatory, for her not to wear a
veil. It is quite in order for the Bride to wear white,
but she usually only has one attendant, not a flock
of bridesmaids. (If an attendant is herself a married
woman, she is called a matron-of-honour.)

Since the Bride is less formally attired, the Groom
and his men will usually wear lounge suits, not morning dress. The procession is also dispensed with, and
the Bride's attendant joins the Groom and Best Man
at the chancel steps, there to await the arrival of the
Bride, unless the Bride herself also chooses to arrive
early with her father or other male relative and wait
in a front pew for the service to commence.

The Church of England does not permit the remarriage of divorced persons. Although clergymen can be
found who will perform the marriage ceremony upon
such people, it is more usual for a blessing to follow a
civil ceremony. The blessing service, which may also
be used in cases where the marriage is between people
of different religious beliefs, has none of the trappings
described above. The minister will give a brief address
followed by prayers to bless the marriage and sometimes a gospel reading.

Double weddings — the marriage of two couples

at the same service before the same minister — are rare, and are usually the result of the decision of two sisters (or occasionally brothers) to marry at the same time. On such occasions, each Groom will have his own Best Man, and each Bride her own retinue of bridesmaids. The elder Groom will be married first. The senior Bride is therefore the one who will marry the elder Groom, regardless of her own age and that of the other Bride. She will enter the church on the right arm of her father, who will have the junior Bride (i.e., the one marrying the younger Groom) on his left. If the two Brides are not sisters, the Bride of the senior Groom and her father come up the aisle first, followed by her bridesmaids. A little way behind them comes the second Bride on her own father's arm, followed by her retinue. After the service, the senior couple should go into the vestry first, sign the register first and start the recession. Each recession party should be complete in itself, ie, the senior Groom, his Bride and their attendants and relatives should lead the way, followed a few paces behind by the junior Groom, his Bride, their attendants and relatives. At the reception afterwards it is usual out of politeness to guests who do not want to spend the rest of the day listening to rambling oratory, for only one of the Best Men to make a speech. Traditionally, the Best man of the senior Groom takes precedence, but it is wise to reach some agreement which recognises the better public speaker.

It is easy to imagine that such events require an enormous amount of organisation, and that one of the reasons for their rarity is the number of things that can go wrong. One example of this was the double wedding of the brothers Darren and Dean Pratt to sisters Christine and Karen Sear. Most of the two hundred and fifty friends and relatives who attended the service addressed their presents to Mr and Mrs D. Pratt, with the predictable result that the couples' first task on returning from their honeymoons was to sort out who got what, and from whom.

When triplets Lesley, Jackie and Andrea Griffiths had a triple wedding, the Brides' mother, with admirable foresight, avoided the possibility of mistaken identity by giving each girl a trimming of pearl studs, satin or lace for their otherwise identical cream silk wedding gowns. Fortunately, the three Grooms, Ian Brightman, Christopher Carlin and David Moreton, all ended up with the right triplet.

Roman Catholic Weddings

There are two forms of marriage in the Roman Catholic church: marriage celebrated during Mass and marriage celebrated outside Mass. The church calendar forbids the former during Lent and between the first Sunday in Advent and 26th December. If one of the parties is a non-Roman Catholic, it is still possible for the full Nuptial Mass to be celebrated with dispensation from the priest. Marriage during Mass is, however, unavailable to those who have not been baptised.

In 'mixed' marriages, the Roman Catholic party has to undertake to avoid falling away from the faith and to do everything possible to ensure that all children of the union are baptised, brought up and educated as Roman Catholics. The priest must be able to sign a statement that in his opinion the non-Catholic party will not oppose the implementation of this undertaking. Consequently, it will usually be necessary for both parties to attend preparatory meetings with the priest, at which several topics will be touched upon, some directly pertaining to the forthcoming marriage, some of a more general nature. Roman Catholic marriages normally take place in Roman Catholic churches, but dispensation can be granted in certain circumstances.

Divorced persons are not allowed to remarry in a Roman Catholic church. However, some forms of marriage are not recognised by Roman Catholicism, and others do not comply with church law (e.g., marriage in a civil register office); therefore it is sometimes possible to obtain from the church a declaration of nullity of a previous marriage.

Both Marriage during Mass and Marriage outside Mass begin in the same way:

1 The Entrance Rite
This takes one of two forms. Either the Groom and Best Man stand at the front right-hand pew and await the arrival of the Bridal party, as in the Church of England ceremony; alternatively (and more unusually) the Groom, Best Man and bridesmaids await the Bride at the door of the church. The priest greets both parties at the door and then leads the procession to the altar.

2 The Liturgy of the Word
This consists of one or two scripture readings followed by a responsorial Psalm.

3 The Marriage Rite
The full text of this is contained in *The Complete Rite of Marriage with Nuptial Mass*, published by

the Catholic Truth Society (*see* Useful Addresses). One important difference from Church of England practice for the Best Man to notice is that he should put the ring onto a silver dish where it is blessed by the priest. The Groom then puts the ring on the Bride's finger. If the Groom is to wear a ring too then the process is repeated.

The Prayer of the Faithful (Bidding Prayer) follows, after which the couple and their attendants move to the sacristry for the signing of the civil register.

That concludes Marriage outside Mass. Marriage inside Mass continues thus: the party returns from sacristy to church; the Bride and Groom take their place between the sanctuary rails while Best Man, parents and attendants return to their original positions at the front of the church. Then follows the Liturgy of the Eucharist, during which Holy Communion may be taken by any member of the congregation who wishes to do so. At the end of the Mass, the recession is led by the Bride and Groom in the usual way.

Jewish Weddings

The ceremony takes place under a *chuppah*. This is a canopy symbolising the couple's married home. It is not in itself a holy place, and may therefore be set up out of doors. Nevertheless, most Jewish weddings take place in synagogues, where it is compulsory to have a head covering. Synagogues will have available paper skullcaps (*yarmulkes* or *kipahs*) for those who do not have their own. The Bride (or *Kallah*) wears a veil which the Groom (*Chatan*) lifts just before they

60

go under the *chuppah*. This is to make sure that he is marrying the right woman, and recalls Genesis 29, in which Jacob was tricked into marrying Leah instead of her younger sister Rachel.

The Marriage Service used in the Reform Synagogues of Great Britain begins with Psalm 84:

How lovely where Your presence dwells
    Lord of all creation.
My soul is longing, pining
    for the courts of the Lord.
My heart and my flesh sing out
    to the living God.

Even a sparrow finds a home
    and a swallow her own nest
    in which to lay her young -
    such are Your altars, Lord of all creation,
    my ruler and my God.

Happy are those who live in Your house
    and can always praise You.
Happy the pilgrim inspired by You,
    they journey to You in their heart.
They pass through the dry sad valley
    and make it seem a place of springs,
    as if the early rain covered it with
    blessings.
They go from strength to strength
    to appear before God in Zion.

Lord, God of all creation, hear my prayer,
    listen, God of Jacob!
God, our shield, look
    and watch over Your anointed!

For one day in Your courts is better
  than a thousand elsewhere.
I would rather stand at the doorway
  of the house of my God
    than live at ease in the tents of the
    wicked.

For the Lord God is a sun and a shield
  the Lord gives favour and glory.
He will not withhold goodness
  from those who walk in integrity.
Lord of all creation,
  happy the man who trusts in You!

This is followed by Psalm 100:

Shout to the Lord all the earth,
  serve the Lord with joy,
    come before Him with singing.

Know that the Lord is God.
  It is He who made us and we are His,
    His own people and the flock of His pasture.

Come into His gates with thanks,
  into His courts with praise,
    thank Him, bless His name.

For the Lord is good,
  His love is everlasting
    and His faithfulness for all generations.

Then the rabbi shall say:

'Blessed are those who come in the name of
the Lord! We bless you from the house of the
Lord. May He who is supreme above all, who is

blessed above all – may He bless the bridegroom and the bride.'

Then the rabbi shall say one of the following three prayers:

A 'Lord, at the quietness of this time, and in the holiness of this place, give Your blessing to Your children. You have given them youth with its hopes and love with its dreams. May these come true through their faith in each other and their trust in You. Let them be devoted to each other, and as the years go by, teach them how great is the joy that comes from sharing, and how deep the love that grows with giving. May Your presence dwell among them in the warmth of their love, in the kindness of their home, and in their charity for others.'

B 'Lord, who taught men and women to help and serve each other in marriage, and lead each other into happiness, bless this covenant of affection, these promises of truth. Protect and care for the bridegroom and bride as they go through life together. May they be loving companions, secure in their devotion which deepens with the passing years. In their respect and honour for each other may they find their peace, and in their affection and tenderness their happiness. May Your presence be in their homes and in their hearts.'

C 'Lord our God, we stand before Your holiness, and in quietness thank You for bringing us to this time. May your love protect *N.* and *N.* who ask You to bless them. They ask Your blessing not for themselves alone but for each other, and for their life together, for in Your blessing is loyalty and devotion, love and trust. Be with them Lord, so that they may know true happiness and bring joy to all who love them. Let them honour You, and so bring honour to themselves. Blessed are You, who teaches mankind the way to happiness.'

The rabbi continues:

'Blessed are You, Lord our God, king of the universe, who creates the fruit of the vine. Blessed are You, Lord our God, king of the universe, who makes us holy through doing His commands, and who makes His people Israel holy by the ceremony of the *chuppah* and the sanctity of marriage.

'Do you *N.* enter into this holy covenant of affection and truth to take *N.* to be your wife in the sight of God and man? And do you faithfully promise to be a true and devoted husband to her?

'Do you *N.* enter into this holy covenant of affection and truth to take *N.* to be your husband in the sight of God and man? And do you faithfully promise to be a true and devoted wife to him?'

The Groom places a gold ring without a stone on the Bride's finger, and as he does so says:

'By this ring you are married to me in holiness according to the law of Moses and Israel.'

Nowadays, it is increasingly common for the woman to reciprocate by giving the man a ring of her own. Whether or not she does this, she will say:

'And you are married to me in holiness according to the law of Moses and Israel.'

Finally the seven benedictions of *nissuim (Sheva Berakahot)* are recited:

'Blessed are You, Lord our God, king of the universe, who creates the fruits of the vine.

'Blessed are You, Lord our God, king of the universe, who created everything for His glory.

'Blessed are You, Lord our God, king of the universe, who forms mankind.

'Blessed are You, Lord our God, king of the universe, who formed mankind in His own image, to be like Him, to imitate Him and to resemble Him, and prepared from mankind and for mankind a constant sharing and renewal. Blessed are You Lord, who forms mankind.

'Let Zion, deprived of her young, rise up again and cry out for joy as her children are gathered around her in happiness. Blessed are You Lord, who gives joy to Zion through her children.

'Give these, companions in love, great happiness, the happiness of Your creatures in Eden long ago. May Your children be worthy to create a Jewish home, that honours You and honours them.

Blessed are You Lord, who rejoices the Bridegroom and the Bride.

'Blessed are You, Lord our God, king of the universe, who created joy and happiness, bridegroom and bride, love and companionship, peace and friendship. Soon, O Lord our God, may the sound of happiness and rejoicing be heard in the towns of Judah and in the streets of Jerusalem, the voice of the bridegroom and the voice of the bride. Blessed are You Lord, who causes the bridegroom to rejoice with the bride.'

The ceremony concludes with Psalm 150:

'Praise the Lord!

'Praise God in His holy place.
    Praise Him in His mighty heavens.
Praise Him for His powerful deeds.
    Praise Him for His surpassing greatness.

'Praise Him with the *shofar* blast.
    Praise Him with the lyre and harp.
Praise Him with drums and dancing.
    Praise Him with lute and pipe.

'Praise Him with the clash of cymbals.
    Praise Him with the clanging cymbals.
Let everything that has breath
    praise the Lord.

'Praise the Lord!'

After this the couple ascend the *Bimah* (a raised platform) where they sign the *kettubah* (the marriage contract) using their Jewish names.

In some communities, the custom prevails of the Bride walking seven times around the Groom before the ceremony proper begins. This is a reference to Jeremiah 31 xxii, 'a woman shall compass a man', and to the seven places in the Old Testament where the phrase 'when a man takes a wife' is used. It is also customary to recite the blessings of *erusin* and *nissuim* over a cup of wine, from which both Bride and Groom drink, and for the Groom to trample glass underfoot, in a symbolic gesture of mourning for the destruction of the Temples in Jerusalem. As the glass breaks, all say aloud '*mazel tov*' ('best wishes').

It was formerly customary to prepare a marriage feast for each day of the following week ('the seven days of feasting') during which the seven benedictions are repeated at table. This practice persists among the Orthodox.

The Best Man at a Jewish wedding is usually the Groom's brother, close relative or best friend. It is very rare for a non-Jew to be asked to fulfil this role. Indeed, Orthodox and Conservative rabbis may actually forbid it. If it is to happen, it will most likely happen under the auspices of the Reform synagogues, where the ceremony may be in Hebrew or in English or in both. At the reception, the Best Man proposes the first toast, to the couple.

Nonconformist Weddings

The term 'Nonconformist' is applied to those churches which refused to conform or subscribe to the Act of Uniformity in 1662, and to Protestants separated from the Church of England. In practice, the word is most often used to describe Baptists and Methodists.

The minister cannot proceed with the wedding ceremony until he is in possession of a valid certificate or certificates (with or without licence) relating to the marriage. It is therefore necessary in the first instance to obtain a Superintendent Registrar's certificate in accordance with the preliminary procedure required for the civil wedding (see 'Where and When Can You Marry?' in Chapter I). In cases where only one party is a Nonconformist, it is permitted, on request, for two ceremonies to take place in churches of different denominations, and both ceremonies are valid as long as they take place on the same day.

Every such ceremony must by law contain the following declaration, to be made in turn by the Groom and then by the Bride:

> 'I call upon these persons here present
> to witness that I, *N.*, do take thee, *N.*,
> to be my lawful wedded wife/husband.'

The Best Man at such weddings should familiarise himself with the details of the service (which, though similar to that of the Church of England, will differ in points of detail) and with the sort of ambience that the couple and their co-religionists hope to create. These weddings are often much simpler than Anglican and Roman Catholic marriages, and are sometimes relatively austere: there might, for example, be no alcohol served at the reception. Fortunately, Nonconformist ministers usually request a wedding rehearsal at which such matters may be clarified.

Quaker Weddings

Quakers (members of the Religious Society of Friends) marry without any of the pageantry associated with the religions so far described. There is no wedding ring, no music and usually no Best Man. Just in case someone is called upon to fulfil this role, here is the form of words used in the ceremony.

Each party shall say to the other (the man first):

'Friends, I take this my friend N., to be my wife/husband, promising through divine assistance, to be unto her/him a loving and faithful husband/wife, so long as we both on earth shall live.'

The declaration may be prefaced with such words as 'In the presence of the Lord', or 'In the fear of the Lord and in the presence of this assembly'. The phrase 'through divine assistance' may be replaced with the words 'with God's help'. The phrase 'as long as we both on earth shall live' may be replaced with the words 'until it shall please the Lord to separate us'.

If, because of an impediment of speech or for some other reason, either of the parties is unable to make the declaration distinctly, then the registering officer present at the marriage shall read the declaration aloud and the parties shall signify their assent to its terms in some previously agreed manner.

Humanist Weddings

A Humanist ceremony is one in which you 'declare' your relationship, thus establishing a common law marriage. This may appeal to couples who want to mark their nuptials with some form of occasion but who do not feel strong bonds of affiliation to any of the established churches.

The Humanists' concern is for the human relationship in marriage, not for its legal status. (The declaration expresses not vows but 'aspirations': although we hope to achieve, we realise that we may not.) If however you do wish such a marriage to be legally binding, it is necessary to incorporate the form of words used in the civil marriage in the register office, and for it to be spoken in the presence of a registrar or clergyman (Unitarian Church ministers will often officiate at such weddings). Apart from that, you may choose the words from any source you like, even write your own script. A booklet called *To Love And To Cherish*, published by the British Humanist Association, (*see* Useful Addresses), makes some splendid suggestions. Here are two examples. The first is from *Memories of Childhood and Youth* by Albert Schweitzer:

'We are each a secret to the other. To know one another cannot mean to know everything about each other; it means to feel mutual affection and confidence, and to believe in one another. We must not try to force our way into the personality of another. To analyse others is a rude commencement, for there is a modesty of the soul which we must recognise just as we do that of the body. No one has a right to say to another: "Because we belong to each other as we do, I have a right to know all your thoughts." Not even a mother may treat a child in that way. All demands of this sort are foolish and unwholesome. In this matter giving is the only valuable process; it is only giving that stimulates. Impart as much as you can of your spiritual being to those who are on the road with you, and accept as something precious what comes back to you from them.'

The second is taken from an American Indian ceremony:

> 'Now you will feel no rain, for each of you
>   will be shelter for the other.
> Now you will feel no cold, for each of you
>   will be warmth to the other.
> Now there is no more loneliness.
> Now you are two persons, but there is only
>   one life before you.
> Go now to your dwelling to enter into the
>   days of your life together.
> And may your days be good and long upon
>   the earth.'

Some Unfortunate Mishaps

No account of the wedding ceremony would be complete without reference to one of the most common mishaps that can befall a Best Man: that he'll end up married to one or the other of the happy couple by mistake.

Phil Brown of Liverpool glanced at his marriage certificate and got a nasty shock to discover that Jill, with whom he had been living since his wedding fourteen years previously, was not his wife after all. Because of a clerical error on the certificate, he was in fact married to Ray Leadbetter, his Best Man.

It wasn't so bad for Kathy Weatherall of Bolton,

who noticed a similar mistake in the car on the way from the ceremony to the reception: at least she was married to someone of the opposite sex. But it wasn't to her fiancé Tony Williams — it was to his brother, Roger, the Best Man.

What might have been the worst wedding day disaster story of recent years was turned into a memorable triumph by a quick-witted vicar. When Lynn Platt married Trevor Bond two days after the terrible storms which tore through southern England on the night of 15th October 1987, the church in Essex had no electricity for heating, lighting or organ. And yet, with the serviceman's genius for improvisation, the Reverend Peter Spencer conducted the ceremony by candlelight and persuaded the hundred and twenty guests to hum the Bride's entrance music. Even the rain which poured through a storm-damaged roof onto the congregation could not dampen their enjoyment — a great time was had by all.

V
THE WEDDING SERVICE

Here is the full text of the Form of Solemnization of Matrimony from the Book of Common Prayer. The notes, which may be found at the end of the chapter, indicate where the text differs from that of the Alternative Service Book, 1966. The best known variants are the omission of 'obey' from the marriage vows and a general modernisation of the language. The reader can decide which version he prefers.

Dearly beloved, we are gathered together here in the sight of God, and in the face of this congregation, to join together this Man and this Woman in holy Matrimony; which is an honourable estate, *instituted of God in the time of man's innocency* [1], signifying unto us the mystical union that is betwixt Christ and his Church; which holy estate Christ adorned and beautified with his presence, and the first miracle that he wrought, in Cana of Galilee; and is commended *of Saint Paul* [2] to be honourable among all men: and therefore is not by any to be enterprised, nor taken in hand, unadvisedly, lightly or wantonly, *to satisfy men's carnal lusts and appetites, like brute beasts that have no understanding* [3]; but reverently, discreetly, *advisedly* [4], soberly, and in the fear of God; duly considering the causes for which Matrimony was ordained.

First, it was ordained for the *procreation of children,*

to be [5] brought up in the fear and nurture of the Lord, and to the praise of his holy Name.

Secondly, it was ordained *for a remedy against sin, and to avoid fornication; that such persons as have not the gift of continency might marry, and keep themselves undefiled members of Christ's body* [6].

Thirdly, it was ordained for the mutual society, help, and comfort, that the one ought to have of the other, both in prosperity and adversity. Into which holy estate these two persons present come now to be joined. Therefore if any man can shew any just cause, why they may not lawfully be joined together, let him now speak, or else hereafter for ever hold his peace.

I require and charge you both, as ye will answer at the dreadful day of judgement when the secrets of all hearts shall be disclosed, that if either of you know any impediment, why ye may not be lawfully joined together in Matrimony, ye do now confess it. For be ye well assured, that so many as are coupled together otherwise than God's Word doth allow are not joined together by God; neither is their Matrimony lawful.

N., wilt thou have this Woman to thy wedded wife, to live together *after God's ordinance* [7] in the holy estate of Matrimony? Wilt thou love her, comfort her, honour, and keep her in sickness and in health; and, forsaking all other, keep thee only unto her, so long as ye both shall live?

The Man shall answer 'I will.'

N., wilt thou have this Man to thy wedded husband, to live together *after God's ordinance* [8] in the holy estate of Matrimony? Wilt thou *obey him, and serve him, love,* [9] honour, and keep him in sickness and in health; and, forsaking all other, keep thee only unto him, so long as ye both shall live?

The woman shall answer 'I will.'

Who giveth this Woman to be married to this Man?

I, *N.*, take thee, *N.*, to my wedded wife, to have and to hold from this day forward, for better for worse, for richer for poorer, in sickness and in health, to love and to cherish, till death us do part, according to God's holy *ordinance* [10]; and thereto I *plight* [11] thee my troth.

I, *N.*, take thee, *N.*, to my wedded husband, to have and to hold from this day forward, for better for worse, for richer for poorer, in sickness and in health, to love, *cherish, and to obey* [12], till death us do part, according to God's holy *ordinance* [13]; and thereto I give thee my troth.

With this Ring I thee wed, with my body I thee *worship* [14], and *with all my wordly goods I thee endow* [15]: in the Name of the Father, and of the Son, and of the Holy Ghost. Amen.

Let us pray. O Eternal God, Creator and Preserver of all mankind, Giver of all spiritual grace, the Author of everlasting life; send thy blessing upon these thy servants, this man and this woman, whom we bless in thy Name; that, *as Isaac and Rebecca lived faithfully together, so these persons* [16] may surely perform and keep the vow and covenant betwixt them made (whereof this Ring given and received is a token and pledge), and may ever remain in perfect love and peace together, and live according to the laws; through Jesus Christ our Lord. Amen.

Those whom God hath joined let no man put asunder.

Forasmuch as *N.*, and *N.*, have consented together in holy wedlock, and have witnessed the same before God and this company, and thereto have given and pledged their troth either to other, and have declared the same by giving and receiving of a Ring, and by

joining of hands; I pronounce that they be Man and
Wife together, In the Name of the Father, and of the
Son, and of the Holy Ghost. Amen.

God the Father, God the Son, God the Holy Ghost,
bless, preserve and keep you; the Lord mercifully
with his favour look upon you; and so fill you with
all spiritual benediction and grace, that ye may so
live together in this life, that in the world to come ye
may have life everlasting. Amen.

The Minister shall then say or sing either Psalm 128
or Psalm 67.

PSALM 128 (Beati omnes)

Blessed are all they that fear the Lord:
    and walk in his ways.

For thou shalt eat the labour of thine hands:
    O well is thee, and happy shalt thou be.

Thy wife shall be as the fruitful vine: upon the
    walls of thine house;

Thy children like the olive-branches: round
    about thy table.

Lo, thus shall the man be blessed: that
    feareth the Lord.

The Lord from out of Sion shall so bless thee:
    that thou shalt see Jerusalem in prosperity
    all thy life long;

Yea, that thou shalt see thy children's
    children: and peace upon Israel.

Glory be to the Father, and to the Son:
    and to the Holy Ghost;

As it was in the beginning, is now, and ever
    shall be: world without end. Amen.

PSALM 67 (Deus misereatur)

God be merciful unto us, and bless us;
    and shew us the light of his countenance,

and be merciful unto us.
That thy way be known upon earth:
    thy saving health among all nations.
Let the people praise thee, O God: yea, let
    all the people praise thee.
Then shall the earth bring forth her increase:
    and God, even our own God, shall give us
    his blessing.
God shall bless us: and all the ends of the
    world shall fear him.
Glory be to the Father, and to the Son:
    and to the Holy Ghost;
As it was in the beginning, is now, and ever
    shall be: world without end. Amen.[17]

Then he leads the prayer:

MINISTER: Lord, have mercy upon us.
ANSWER: Christ, have mercy upon us.
MINISTER: Lord, have mercy upon us.
Our Father, which art in heaven, Hallowed by thy Name. Thy kingdom come. Thy will be done, in earth as it is in heaven. Give us this day our daily bread. And forgive us our trespasses, As we forgive them that trespass against us. And lead us not into temptation; But deliver us from evil. Amen.
MINISTER: O Lord, save thy servant, and thy handmaid;
ANSWER: Who put their trust in thee.
MINISTER: O Lord, send them help from this holy place;
ANSWER: And evermore defend them.
MINISTER: Be unto them a tower of strength;
ANSWER: From the face of their enemy.
MINISTER: O Lord, hear our prayer.
ANSWER: And let our cry come unto thee.
MINISTER: O God of *Abraham, God of Isaac, God of Jacob* [18], bless these thy servants, and sow the seed

77

of eternal life in their hearts; that whatsoever in thy holy Word they shall profitably learn, they may in deed fulfil the same. *Look, O Lord, mercifully upon them from heaven, and bless them. And as thou didst send thy blessing upon Abraham and Sarah, to their great comfort, so vouchsafe to send thy blessing upon these thy servants* [19]; *that they* [20] obeying thy will, and alway being in safety under thy protection, may abide in thy love unto their lives' end; through Jesus Christ our Lord. Amen.'

This Prayer next following shall be omitted, where the Woman is past child-bearing.

'O Merciful Lord, and heavenly Father, by whose gracious gift mankind is increased; *We beseech thee, assist with thy blessing these two persons, that they may both be fruitful in procreation of children, and also live together so long in godly love and honesty,*[21] that they may see their children christianly and virtuously brought up, to thy praise and honour; through Jesus Christ our Lord. Amen.'

O God, *who by thy mighty power hast made all things of nothing; who also (after other things set in order) didst appoint, that out of man (created after thine own image and similitude) woman should take her beginning; and, knitting them together, didst teach* [22] that it should never be lawful to put asunder those whom thou by Matrimony hadst made one: *O God, who* [23] hast consecrated the state of Matrimony to such an excellent mystery, that in it is signified and represented the spiritual marriage and unity betwixt Christ and his Church; Look mercifully upon these thy servants, that both this man may love his wife, according to thy Word, (as Christ did love his spouse the Church, who gave himself for it, loving and cherishing it even as his own flesh,) and also

78

that this woman may be loving and amiable, *faithful and obedient* [24] to her husband; and in all quietness, sobriety and peace, be a follower of holy and godly matrons. O Lord, bless them both, and grant them to inherit thy everlasting kingdom; through Jesus Christ our Lord. Amen.

Then the Priest shall say,

Almighty God, *who at the beginning did create our first parents, Adam and Eve, and did sanctify and join them together in marriage* [25] pour upon you the riches of his grace, sanctify and bless you, that ye may please him both in body and soul, and live together in holy love unto your lives' end. Amen.

Finally, if there is to be no Sermon, the Book of Common Prayer directs that the Minister should read the following:

All ye that are married, or that intend to take the holy estate of Matrimony upon you, hear what the holy Scripture doth say as touching the duty of husbands towards their wives, and wives towards their husbands.

Saint Paul, in his Epistle to the Ephesians, the fifth Chapter, doth give this commandment to all married men; Husbands, love your wives, even as Christ also loved the Church, and gave himself for it, that he might sanctify and cleanse it with the washing of water, by the Word; that he might present it to himself a glorious Church, not having spot, or wrinkle, or any such thing; but that it should be holy, and without blemish. So ought men to love their wives as their own bodies. He that loveth his wife loveth himself: for no man ever yet hated his own flesh, but nourisheth and cherisheth it, even as the Lord of the Church: for we are members of his body, of his flesh, and of his bones. For this cause shall a man leave his father and mother, and shall be joined unto his wife; and they two shall be one flesh. This is a great mystery; but I speak concerning Christ and the Church. Nevertheless, let every one of you in particular so love his wife, even as himself.

Likewise the same Saint Paul, writing to the Colossians, speaketh thus to all men that are married; Husbands, love your wives and be not bitter against them.

Hear also what Saint Peter, the Apostle of Christ, who was himself a married man, saith unto them that are married; Ye husbands, dwell with your wives according to knowledge; giving honour unto the wife, as unto the weaker vessel, and as being heirs together of the grace of life, that your prayers be not hindered.

Hitherto ye have heard the duty of the husband towards the wife. Now likewise, ye wives, hear and learn your duties toward your husbands, even as it is plainly set forth in holy Scripture.

Saint Paul, in the aforenamed Epistle to the Ephesians, teacheth you thus; Wives, submit yourselves unto your own husbands, as unto the Lord. For the husband is the head of the wife, even as Christ is the head of the Church: and he is the Saviour of the body. Therefore as the Church is subject unto Christ, so let the wives be to their own husbands in every thing. And again he saith, Let the wife see that she reverence her husband.

And in his Epistle to the Colossians, Saint Paul giveth you this short lesson; Wives, submit yourselves unto your own husbands, as it is fit in the Lord.

Saint Peter also doth instruct you very well, thus saying; Ye wives, be in subjection to your own husbands; that, if any obey not the Word, they also may without the Word be won by the conversation of the wives; while they behold your chaste conversation coupled with fear. Whose adorning, let it not be that outward adorning of plaiting the hair, and of wearing of gold, or of putting on of apparel; but let it be the hidden man of the heart, in that which is not corruptible; even the ornament of a meek and quiet spirit, which is in the sight of God of great price. For after this manner in the old time the holy women also, who trusted in God, adorned themselves, being in subjection unto their own husbands; even as Sarah obeyed Abraham, calling him lord; whose daughters ye are as long as ye do well, and are not afraid with any amazement.'

That concludes the wedding service as given in the Book of Common Prayer.

In the Alternative Service Book 1966, the form of words from the end of the blessing is as follows:

Let us pray. O Almighty Lord, and everlasting God, vouchsafe, we beseech thee, to direct, sanctify, and govern, both our hearts and bodies, in the ways of thy laws, and in the works of thy commandments; that through thy most mighty protection, both here and ever, we may be preserved in body and soul; through our Lord and Saviour Jesus Christ. Amen.

The blessing of God Almighty, the Father, the Son, and the Holy Ghost, be amongst you and remain with you always. Amen.

The Collect

O God our Father, who by thy holy Apostle hast taught us that love is the fulfilling of the law: Grant to these thy servants that, loving one another, they may continue in thy love unto their lives' end; through Jesus Christ our Lord, who liveth and reigneth with

81

thee in the unity of the Holy Ghost, one God world
without end. Amen.

The Epistle (Ephesians 3, xiv)

For this cause I bow my knees unto the Father of
our Lord Jesus Christ, of whom the whole family in
heaven and earth is named, that he would grant you,
according to the riches of his glory, to be strength-
ened with might by his Spirit in the inner man; that
Christ may dwell in your hearts by faith; that ye,
being rooted and grounded in love, may be able to
comprehend with all saints what is the breadth, and
length, and depth, and height; and to know the love
of Christ, which passeth knowledge, that ye might be
filled with all the fulness of God.

The Gospel (St John 15, ix)

As the Father hath loved me, so have I loved you:
continue ye in my love. If ye keep my commandments,
ye shall abide in my love; even as I have kept my
Father's commandments, and abide in His love. These
things have I spoken unto you, that my joy might
remain in you, and that your joy might be full. This
is my commandment, That ye love one another, as I
have loved you.

Notes

1 Alternative Version: 'instituted of God himself'
2 AV: 'in Holy Writ'
3 AV omits this
4 AV omits this
5 AV: 'increase of mankind according to the will of God,
and that children might be'
6 AV: 'in order that the natural instincts and affections,
implanted by God, should be hallowed and directed
aright; that those who are called of God to this holy

estate, should continue therein in pureness of living'

7 & 8 AV: 'according to God's law'

9 AV: 'love him, comfort him'

10 AV: 'law'

11 AV: 'give'

12 AV: 'and to cherish'

13 AV: 'law'

14 AV: 'honour'

15 AV: 'all my worldly goods with thee I share'

16 AV: 'living faithfully together, they'

17 AV also offers Psalm 37, iii-vii (*Spera in Domino*):

> Put thou thy trust in the Lord, and be doing good:
>   dwell in the land, and verily thou shalt be fed.
>
> Delight thou in the Lord: and He shall give thee
>   thy heart's desire.
>
> Commit thy way unto the Lord, and put thy trust in
>   Him: and he shall bring it to pass.
>
> He shall make thy righteousness as clear as the light:
>   and thy just dealing as the noon-day.
>
> Hold thee still in the Lord: and abide patiently
>   upon Him.
>
> Glory be to the Father, and to the Son; and to the
>   Holy Ghost;
>
> As it was in the beginning, is now, and ever shall be:
>   world without end. Amen.

18 AV: 'our fathers'

19 AV omits this

20 AV 'that so'

21 AV: 'bestow, we beseech thee, upon these two persons
the heritage and gift of children; and grant'

22 AV: 'who hast taught us'

23 AV: 'and'

24 AV: 'and faithful'

25 AV: 'the Father of our Lord Jesus Christ'

VI
THE RECEPTION

A survey conducted by *You and Your Wedding* magazine in 1988 calculated that the average cost of a wedding reception was over £1200; at a society wedding, it might cost nearly ten times that amount. Since this is the largest single item of expenditure at any wedding, it is important to remember exactly who foots the bill. Although the show is put on for the benefit of the Bride and Groom, it is most frequently her parents who pay for it. It is therefore her parents who choose the menu, the wine, the cake and decide the number of guests. They call the tune, and it is to them that everyone present should defer.

The reception is usually held in one of three places: in a hotel hired for the occasion; in the home of the Bride's parents; or in a marquee in their garden. The last is expensive to hire, but does create an agreeably festive atmosphere and saves the house from the battering it will surely otherwise suffer at the hands, feet and cigarette ends of a large number of guests.

The Best Man will find it useful to have at his fingertips the following information about the reception: where it is to be held (obvious enough, you may think, but bear in mind that it will be most helpful if he can provide clear directions from the church); how many people are invited and the names of any VIPs (just in case he will need to preface his speech with 'My lords, ladies and gentlemen'); the estimated time of arrival at the reception after the ceremony; whether the photographer will be present (if not, there should be someone with a camera to record the event); the time of the meal; the seating plan; who will speak; the going-away time. He should also make sure that he knows from whom he may pick up the Telemessages which will have been sent to the Bride's parents' home and which he will have to read out during his speech. In addition, he should find out who will be responsible for collecting up the presents and remnants of wedding cake afterwards to take to the home of the Bride's mother: once again, if no one else will do it, the Best Man should not fail.

On entering the reception, it is traditional for the guests to form a reception line and wait to be introduced to the main participants, who stand together inside the entrance. First they will meet the Bride's mother and father, then the Groom's parents, then the Bride and Groom. The bridesmaids may stand behind the Bride, but this is sometimes felt to be an unnecessary delay in the important task of getting everyone in as quickly as possible. The guests may be introduced by the Best Man or by the Master of Ceremonies (if there is one: often the hotel manager will make himself available for this duty as part of the package); more commonly, however, the guests are left to introduce themselves.

The line should be kept moving. Guests who are meeting the couple's parents for the first time should confine themselves to the briefest salutation and explanation of who they are — 'I'm Oliver Varney, I was at school with Alistair', will probably suffice. 'Delighted to meet you; I've heard a great deal about you', is probably enough from the hosts by way of

The line should be kept moving

reply. Old friends of the family should resist any urge they may feel to take a stroll down memory lane: they should save it for later when the Bride and Groom circulate among the guests. Some authorities hold that guests should not say 'Congratulations' to the Bride, merely wish her 'every happiness'; however, 'Congratulations' is often heard and never seems to cause offence (why should it?). After they have been presented, the guests move on into the hall and receive a welcoming drink, often but not always of champagne.

If the wedding reception is a buffet, after the last guest has been introduced to the reception party, the Bride and Groom should move to be the first to be served with food, and the guests should take this as their cue to follow suit. If it is a full sit-down meal, of course, everyone will wait until all the guests are seated.

At a sit-down meal, there is usually a seating plan for the guests to follow. At the top table, a typical arrangement would be:

| BEST MAN | GROOM'S FATHER | BRIDE'S MOTHER | GROOM | BRIDE | BRIDE'S FATHER | GROOM'S MOTHER | CHIEF BRIDESMAID |

Note that only one side of the top table is occupied, so that the main characters can see and be seen easily. If the church minister and his wife attend the reception, they should also be seated on the top table. Otherwise much will depend upon family feuds (no family is without them), divorces and the cordiality of various parties to one another. Bearing in mind all these variables, the seating plan here is only a suggestion.

Grace may be said before the meal, but nowadays this is often omitted, unless there is a religious minister present, in which case it should be regarded as obligatory.

After coffee has been served, either the Best Man or

the Toastmaster will call for order and introduce the Bride's father, who will propose a toast to 'the health and happiness of the Bride and Groom'. (This function does not have to be fulfilled by the Bride's father — sometimes it is a godfather or a distinguished friend — but the Bride's father must have first refusal of the job.) He may just stand up, raise his glass and make the toast without any embellishment; usually, however, he will make a short speech. He will talk about his daughter's early years, about his new son-in-law, about their suitability for one another, and wish them every happiness in the future.

When he has finished, the Groom will reply on behalf of himself and the Bride. Whatever he says or does not say, he will be well advised to thank the Bride's mother and father for all their efforts in laying on the reception. He may interrupt his speech to give each of the bridesmaids in turn a small gift; alternatively, he may prefer the Best Man to do this on his behalf during his own speech. The Groom concludes by proposing a toast to the bridesmaids.

Finally, the Best Man replies on behalf of the Bridesmaids. This speech is supposed to be the high point of the reception, an upbeat and amusing address calculated to spread sweetness and light throughout the assembly. Towards the end of it, he should break off to read the Telemessages. Into the normal run of 'All good wishes from Jan and Peter' he may wish to interpolate a spoof or two. In general, most of these are either too louche or too well-known to be amusing. Here is just one example:

'To *N*. (the Bride) from *N*. (the Groom's school)

The Bride should only make the first cut

old boys' football club: "We've tried him in every position, now it's your turn." '

The problem with such chestnuts is finding the right audience: most people have heard them all before, and those who have not are likely to disapprove of them.

After that, the Best Man should conclude with some form of words like '. . . and now it only remains for me to say, on behalf of the bridesmaids, thank you very much', and sit down.

The next stage is the cutting of the cake. The Bride and Groom should together, with the Groom's hand over the Bride's, make one downward incision into the icing. From then on, the caterer takes over

89

and cuts the rest of the cake for distribution among the guests. Anything left over at the end is removed to the Bride's mother's home and sent to friends and relatives who were unable to attend.

That concludes the formal part of the reception. It used to be customary to display the presents for all the guests to see by setting them up on tables covered with white tablecloths and tiered with large boxes. The presents were removed from their packages and identified by white cards bearing the donors' names and addresses. Cheques were banked straightaway for security reasons, but a card headed 'Cheques have been received from. . .' would be displayed to acknowledge the gifts with thanks. Nowadays, however, as the risk of theft has become so great, particularly if the reception is held in a hotel rather than at the home of the Bride's parents, this practice wisely goes by the board.

Some time later, the Bride and Groom will retire separately to change from their wedding clothes into going-away outfits. She will be attended by her bridesmaids, he by his Best Man. On their return in mufti, the car or taxi should be ready for departure. If he has not done so already, the Best Man should now hand over any tickets, money and keys he may have been holding for the Groom. The Bride should throw her bouquet to one of the bridesmaids (tradition has it that the one who catches it will be the next to marry), and the happy couple should leave in short order. The best advice here is, 'if it were done, . . . then 'twere well It were done quickly': long leave-takings can become emotional, and are best avoided.

It may be taken for granted that some of the guests will deface the car in the traditional manner

— old shoes tied to the back bumper, a cardboard sign saying 'Just Married', shaving cream on the back window. It may also be presumed that the Groom will take the whole lot off again as soon as he has got round the corner and is out of sight.

Alternatively, it is increasingly the form for the reception to be followed by an evening function, usually a disco dance. In such case, the above still applies, except of course that the Bride and Groom, after changing their clothes, do not leave, but attend the evening do. Rather than go off on a long journey late at night, they may choose to spend the wedding night at the hotel at which the reception was held. One of the advantages of this extra event is that it gives the Bride and Groom an opportunity to spend more time talking to the guests than would be possible if they left directly after the reception.

VII
THE SPEECHES

It is traditional for three men to make speeches at a wedding reception — they are, in order, the Bride's father, the Groom and the Best Man. The first proposes a toast to the Bride and Groom; the second, a toast to the bridesmaids; the third replies on behalf of the bridesmaids. That is the bare skeleton; the fleshing out may be done in many ways. Some Brides may wish to speak themselves — if so, there is no point of etiquette to prevent them from doing so, and quite rightly.

The Bride's father will usually refer to some happy and amusing incidents in his daughter's childhood, his feelings for his new son-in-law and his son-in-law's parents (assuming, of course, that he can find something favourable to say about any of them!); then he will perhaps proffer some advice on the prerequisites of a happy marriage, and express his confidence that the Bride and Groom will make the effort and not be found wanting.

The Groom's reply (which is on his wife's behalf as well as his own) should thank the Bride's father for his kind remarks and good wishes, and also for laying on the reception. He should not neglect to mention the Bride's mother, too. Moreover, it is usual for him to thank both his parents-in-law for letting him marry their daughter. He should make a point of referring to his own parents ('thank you for having me' is a common joke), and to the bridesmaids, saying how lovely they look.

The Best Man should remember that the ostensible reason for his speech is to reply on behalf of the bridesmaids to the kind remarks made about them by the Groom. Any extra material he works into his speech is a matter for his own judgment. Although no one will think less of the Best Man if he simply stands up, says thank you, raises his glass and sits down again, it is traditional for him to make a few light-hearted remarks of a general nature about the Groom. Many would say this is far easier said than done. To become a proficient public speaker it is necessary to draw upon many other disciplines: oratory is perhaps the most diverse of the arts. It is interesting to reflect that while almost anyone can name great athletes, great painters and great poets, few can summon to mind the name of a great orator. Even if they can think of someone, the chances are that he will be dead. Many who recall admiringly the speeches of Churchill and Aneurin Bevan in the same breath deprecate the skills of Michael Foot and Neil Kinnock. Oratory is the actor's art, but how many actors are good public speakers? It is often remarked that so-and-so is only good with a script; when he tries to express himself, he is stumblingly inarticulate.

It may even be that oratory is the most difficult of all the arts. This may seem odd, since athletics and literature, painting and music require training whereas oratory does not. Yet the source of oratory is knowledge, and knowledge only comes with experience. Experience of what? First and most important, good manners. One polite gesture is not to speak for too long. As a rule of thumb, up to ten minutes may be accounted a compliment to the audience, fifteen minutes a gaffe, twenty minutes a nerve, half an hour a diabolical liberty. Don't drool on like the cure for insomnia, and remember that it is better to sit down and leave people saying 'I wish he'd stood up longer' than to go on until they start murmuring 'why doesn't he sit down?' It is really not necessary for the Best Man to demonstrate the reason for his appointment by cataloguing his every memory of the Groom since nursery school. Everyone present will assume that he and the Groom 'go back a long way': don't rub it in. The secret of being a bore is to say everything.

When it comes to salacious anecdotes and remarks, it is advisable always to err firmly on the side of caution: many people have attended weddings at which the Best Man has made references to the Groom's old flames or to having caught the Bride and Groom in pre-marital flagrante delicto; and wished he hadn't. As Montaigne said, 'No man is exempt from saying silly things; the mischief is to say them deliberately'. A gentleman (and the Groom will dearly hope that he has given the job of Best Man to one of those) will always say what he can. He will also have a pretty good idea of what he cannot say: a wedding speech is not the place for wistful references to the Groom's disappointment at being passed over for a partnership in his firm, or to the reason for his expulsion from public school. It is perhaps permissible to allude to a deceased relative who everyone wishes could have been present at the great day. However, it is often better to leave this to the family: promiscuous expressions of sympathy are not always welcome. Be charming, urbane, humorous. Be in no doubt that it is possible to be amusing without being *risqué*. This

94

Practise until your reflection is bored to tears by you

is not intended as a puritanical blast against blue jokes, merely as a reminder that there are puritans about, and they form a caucus at every wedding in the world. Anyway, there is a time and a place for scatology, and a wedding reception is neither.

Practise your speech in front of the mirror until your reflection is bored to tears by the sight of you — public speaking is like writing: the more easily it comes across to the audience, the harder the preparation that went into it. Don't be shy about working on a few emphatic gestures — remember that the audience will be watching you as well as listening to you. The occasional movement, judiciously used, can be very effective, but don't go too far or you'll end up

95

looking like a 1930s dictator in full rant. Cast a critical eye over your deportment — don't loll or stoop, don't talk down into your chest. Stand up straight and aim your voice at the back of the hall.

Rehearsing into a tape recorder is an excellent method of preparation — you'll get a clear idea of how your every intonation sounds and be able to time your speech exactly. If you record each new 'take' over the last, you will soon discover how great can be the difference between the shortest and the longest time it takes you to recite the same speech.

A tape recorder will also give you a fresh ear for your vocal intonations — fascinating they are too, once you have got over the initial embarrassment of hearing your own voice on tape. Remember that you should speak more slowly and more loudly than in normal conversation. The former applies even to the most naturally ponderous speaker, the latter even to those who will speak on the day with the assistance of a microphone.

On the day, try not to loosen your tie — it will make you look drunk. Don't shuffle your feet, or you'll look like the man at the supermarket check-out who can't pay for the goods in his trolley. You should either have a few headings on cards as a prompt or else the whole speech written out in front of you. The first method is for those who are really quite confident about their speech; the second is a safety net for those who fear that they might dry up completely. Of course no one should read the whole speech from the page — that cannot fail to be dull. Although the speech should not be learned by heart, it should be well enough known for only occasional glances at the text to be necessary. In other words, the text in front of you should be used as a walking stick, not as a crutch. (Incidentally, space your writing so that there's no danger of losing your place when you do refer to your notes.)

Don't try too hard to be original. Apart from the fact that there is no new thing under the sun, originality, even if you can achieve it, is something which will be admired but not necessarily liked. It gives the appearance of benefitting the speaker himself rather than the people about whom it is said or those before whom it is paraded. Remember, too, that jokes at the Groom's expense should be about his successes, not about his failures: the only failure that is humorous is your own.

Don't depart from the language of everyday life — nothing will spoil your speech more quickly than if you strive to come across as cleverer than you are. Don't make in-jokes either, for even if you know that two people in the audience will twig, remember the majority: at best you won't get a big laugh, and at worst you may alienate everybody. The best advice is to let good jokes hang with the plumpest blackberries, out of the way, at the back of hedge and to remember that it is probably wise not to make any double entendres about the prick you got while reaching for them.

If all this makes speech-making sound almost impossibly difficult, don't despair: everyone, after all, will be on your side. As you stand up to speak and your life flashes before you, look at the expectant faces and think of exactly what it is they are expecting — wit, sincerity, tact and brevity. If you can't deliver any of the first three, you can still be an enormous success with the fourth.

It is common for reluctant public speakers as they approach the end of their notes suddenly to start to feel that it's not such an ordeal after all, perhaps they could go on a bit longer. *Advice:* forget it. Sit down, wallow in the applause, and even if you can't congratulate yourself on a job well done, you can at least thank your stars you got through it.

VIII
IT'S UNLUCKY TO BE SUPERSTITIOUS

There are many superstitions associated with weddings: here is a résumé of some of the better known and more outlandish. The reader may take them or leave them — in most cases, preferably the latter.

The signs that foretell an imminent marriage are these: if a live coal falls at your feet out of a fire; if you snuff out a candle accidentally or if you have recently been given two teaspoons in one saucer. On the other side of the coin, if you sit on a table you will never marry; if you are three times a bridesmaid, you will never be a Bride.

If you want to divine the date of your wedding, you should wait until Shrove Tuesday, make a pancake, give it to a farmyard cockerel and count the number of hens that come to help him eat it. Each hen represents a month that will pass before your marriage. (*Important*: do not make a second pancake before the cock has been given the first, or the omen is useless.)

In some areas it was counted unlucky for a woman to marry a man whose surname began with the same letter as her own. This belief comes from the saying:

'Change the name and not the letter
Change for the worse, not for the better'.

Dates for Weddings

In Great Britain, Friday is supposedly the most
ill-omened day for marriage (*cf* Germany, where it
is Wednesday). The old verse runs:

> 'Monday for wealth,
> Tuesday for health,
> Wednesday the best day of all.
> Thursday for losses,
> Friday for crosses,
> And Saturday for no luck at all.'

(The deficiency of the rhyme may be taken as symp-
tomatic of the feeble-mindedness of the content.)

The worst month for marrying is May: 'From
marriages in May, all the bairns die and decay';
'Marry in May, rue for aye'. Plutarch explains this by
saying that May is the month for making offerings to
the dead and wearing mourning. If you must marry
in May, the least ill-omened dates are 2nd, 4th, 12th
and 23rd. The worst date in all the calendar is Friday
13th May. Other bad times are Lent ('Marry in Lent
and you'll live to repent'), Advent and Easter Week. St
Swithin's Day (15th July) and St Thomas's Day (21st
December) are also often avoided. Childermas (28th
December) is extremely inauspicious — some say that
marriage should not be entered into on the day of the
week in which the previous Childermas has fallen.

One should not marry between a full moon and a
new moon. To marry on the wane of the moon means
that the luck of the marriage will also wane. Neither

100

should you marry on your own birthday or on that of your spouse, unless you were both born on the same day, in which case that is the most auspicious day of all. For all other couples, the best day for marriage is 29th February.

Other good times to get married are at the start of the year ('Marry when the year is new, /Always loving, always true') and in autumn, because of its association with fecundity:

> 'Marry in September's shine,
> Your living will be rich and fine.
> If in October you do marry,
> Love will come but riches tarry.
> If you wed in bleak November,
> Only joy will come remember.
> When December's showers fall fast,
> Marry and true love will last.'

On the Wedding Day

The Bride and Groom must not see each other before the ceremony. It was not ever thus: until the beginning of the twentieth century, 'walking weddings' were still common practice. The Bride would lead the way to the church accompanied by the Best Man, while the Groom would follow with the bridesmaid(s). On the way back, the married couple would lead the way, followed by the retinue. (In those days, however, it was often customary to exclude the couple's parents from the procession and/or the ceremony.)

The Bride should wear white or silver or blue or pink or gold or grey or fawn. Black should never be

101

worn because of its association with death, and the same goes for purple. Green is also an unlucky colour because it is supposed to indicate that mourning will be worn in the near future. Yellow means that you are forsworn, brown that your husband will never be wealthy.

The Bride should wear something old, something new, something borrowed and something blue. A veil borrowed from the Bride's mother often satisfies two of these requirements. Blue (most often worn in the garter) signifies constancy. (Some say that everything should be new, to signify entry into a new state of life.)

The Bride should not make her own wedding dress: even professional dressmakers often observe this tradition. The dress should not be completed in one go, nor completed before the wedding day. The Bride should not wear the complete outfit before the day.

Put your right arm into your clothing first; put on your left stocking and shoe before the right; put both legs into your trousers at the same time (another good reason for not holding the Stag Party the night before).

The Bride should not look at her reflection in the mirror while wearing the complete wedding dress: to do so before the ceremony will prevent the marriage.

In Wales, the Bride used to put a silver sixpence in her shoe for a happy and prosperous life.

If you find a piece of coal in the road, rejoice: fortune is smiling upon you. Pick it up, spit on it, throw it over your left shoulder, walk on without looking back and make a wish.

To pass a funeral procession or even an empty hearse coming in the opposite direction is a bad omen: avert it by turning round and following it for a little way.

A horseshoe is always lucky, because it is a combination of iron, a magical metal, and fire, a mysterious element. If you find one en route to the ceremony, the marriage is blessed. Failing that, one may be tied to the back of the going-away car, but it must be a genuine horseshoe from a real horse.

Carry a small handful of salt in your pocket so that if you meet the Devil on the road you can throw it over your left shoulder into his face and blind him. Some folklorists hold that the reason the Bride has attendant bridesmaids dressed in the same style is to confuse the Devil if he comes to steal the Bride for himself.

It is lucky for the Bride to see a rainbow, and doubly lucky for her to see both ends of it. Needless to say, fine weather is taken as a good omen.

Animals play a prominent part in the superstitions of marriage. For example, it is lucky if either Bride or Groom meets an elephant on the way to the church. If a cat sneezes near a bride, her marriage will be a happy one. A black cat crossing your path is a good omen; a white cat is a bad one, as is a pig. In Scotland, it is unlucky for the couple if a dog passes between them on their wedding day.

It is unlucky if the Bride's car fails to start, or if the wedding party enters the church through the lychgate or the north door (which are normally reserved for funerals). An open grave in the church-yard is also a particularly bad sign. But if one of these things befalls you, don't despair: the omens can be averted simply by crossing your fingers.

It is unlucky if the Bride does not weep bitterly on her wedding day.

Meeting a chimney sweep is a good omen. He should offer his congratulations and walk a little way alongside the procession. Some chimney sweeps hire themselves out for this very purpose. At competitive rates they turn out in top hats and tails, hands and faces smeared with soot. Legend has it that on the day of the marriage of Princess Elizabeth and Prince Philip in 1947, the Prince rushed from Buckingham Palace to shake hands with a passing sweep.

When the Bride is set down at the door of the church, the horses or car which brought her should drive on before turning round: for them to turn straightaway is bad luck.

At the Wedding
Orange blossom is a particularly auspicious symbol of luck and fertility, but whatever the choice of

A lucky omen?

flower, never give an even number of blooms in a bouquet.

The Bride departing for her honeymoon should stand at the head of the stairs and throw her right shoe (the one she married in) among the unmarried guests. Whoever catches it will be the next to marry. (The same applies to her bouquet.)

It is unlucky for a stone to roll across the path of a newly-married couple.

Guests should throw shoes after the newly-weds as they leave for the honeymoon. This is supposed to be lucky, doubly so if one of them gets hit. (Whether one of them being knocked unconscious counts as a propitious augury is not recorded.)

At Welsh weddings it was the practice for the Best Man to give the Bride a slice of bread and butter to eat before the cake was cut; its smallness and daintiness ensured that the Bride's children would have small, pretty mouths.

In most communities, it was counted unlucky if the Bride had elder unmarried sisters. To banish the omen, the sisters had to dance at the wedding without shoes. In Devon in bygone days, a small furze faggot was placed across the threshold of the Bride's home. On her return from the wedding, the elder sister had to step over it, thus overcoming the obstacle to her own marriage. This was known as 'dancing the furze faggot'.

The Wedding Cake
The first slice must be cut by the Bride, or else the marriage will be childless.

If the Groom is a soldier, the couple should cut the cake with his sword.

For a guest to refuse a slice of cake would bring bad luck to both himself and the couple.

The couple should keep a slice for themselves, until the christening of their first child (it will also help to keep the husband faithful).

If a piece of wedding cake is put under the pillow

of a maiden before she goes to bed, she will dream of her future husband. If it is drawn through the Bride's wedding ring either three times or nine times (depending on the locality) and then placed under a pillow, either a man or a woman may dream of their future spouse.

The Wedding Ring

If a woman loses her wedding ring, she will lose her husband.

If a wedding ring wears thin or comes to pieces or breaks, one or other partner will die.

In Ireland it was commonly believed that a marriage was not legal unless it was solemnised with a gold ring. In many poorer areas it was the custom of the priest or registrar to hire out a golden ring to those who could not afford one themselves.

For a girl to divine whether or not she was to be married, she would take a tumbler of south-running water, borrow the wedding ring of a happily married woman, and suspend it by a hair from her own head over the glass, holding the hair between a finger and thumb of her left hand. If the ring hit itself against the rim of the glass she would never marry. If the ring turned quickly round, she would be married. If it turned slowly, she would have two husbands.

Some say that the wedding ring is worn on the third finger of the left hand because a vein runs from there directly to the heart. There is no such vein. A likelier explanation of the custom is that the third finger cannot be fully extended on its own, whereas every other finger can be, and a ring cannot easily fall off a crooked finger.

After the Wedding

If a hen is taken into the couple's new home and made to cackle, it will bring them good luck.

Blood Weddings

These are for people who cannot marry by more conventional means. The procedure is as follows: cut the upper side of your forearm with a razor blade about two inches above the wrist (not deeply, and not underneath). Make a similar incision in your partner's opposite arm — right for the male, left for the female — then hold your arms together, blood on blood, for one minute. Either keep the razor blade or throw it on the fire. (*Warning*: only a magician can loose this bond.)

IX
BEST BEST MEN

Prince Andrew married Sarah Ferguson on 23 July 1986, at Westminster Abbey. His supporter was Prince Edward.

Jeffrey Archer married Mary Doreen Weeden on 11 July 1966 at St Mary the Virgin, Oxford. Best Man: Adrian Metcalfe. Ceremony conducted by the Rev Leslie Styler, Chaplain of Brasenose College.

Anthony Armstrong Jones married Princess Margaret on 6 May 1960 at Westminster Abbey. Best Man: Dr Roger Gilliatt.

George Best married Angela MacDonald Janes on 24 January 1978 in Las Vegas. Best Man: Bobby McAlinden, Best's team-mate in the Los Angeles Aztecs.

David Bowie married Angela Bennett in 1970 at Bromley Register Office, Kent. No Best Man. Witnesses: John Cambridge and Clare Shenstone.

Richard Burton married Sally Hay, a television production assistant, in a ten minute ceremony in the Presidential suite of the Frontier Hotel, Las Vegas. Best Man: Brook Williams. He and Valerie Douglas, Burton's California agent, were the only guests.

Charles, Prince of Wales, married Lady Diana Spencer on 29 July 1981. Supporter: Prince Andrew, the Groom's brother.

G.K. Chesterton married Frances Blogg on 28 June 1901 at St Mary Abbots, Kensington, London. Best Man: Lucian Oldershaw.

Lord Randolph Churchill married Jeanette Jerome on 15 April 1874 at the British Embassy, Paris. Best Man: Francis Knolleys, private secretary to the Prince and Princess of Wales.

Winston Leonard Spenser Churchill married Clementine Hozier on 12 September 1908 at St Margaret's, Westminster, London. No Best Man, but Lloyd George, then one of Churchill's closest political allies, signed the register.

Eric Clapton married Patti Boyd, ex-wife of Beatle George Harrison on 28 March 1979 in Tucson, Arizona. A church wedding with no Best Man. The Groom wore an off-white cowboy hat with matching tuxedo and boots.

Samuel Taylor Coleridge married Sarah Fricker on 4 October 1795 at St Mary Redcliffe, Bristol. Best Man: Josiah Wade, Bristolian tradesman and radical.

Michael Denison married Dulcie Gray in 1939, five days after leaving drama school where they met, by special licence at St Xavier's, Knightsbride, London. Best Man: Maurice Williams, an old school friend who was subsequently killed in the Second World War.

They had a one-night honeymoon in The Dorchester: 'Splendour never far away with Michael'. Then they were off to Aberdeen, where they played opposite each other in Coward's *Hay Fever*, with Stewart Granger as leading man.

Charles Dickens married Catherine Hogarth on 2 April 1836 at St Luke's Chelsea, London. The ceremony was so simple that in later years he could remember nothing about it. Best Man: Thomas Beard, a reporter on the *Morning Herald*.

Benjamin Disraeli married Mrs Mary Anne Wyndham Lewis on 28 August 1838 at St George's, Hanover Square, London. Best Man not recorded, but Henry Bulwer Lytton, diplomat and author, and John Singleton Copley, Baron Lyndhurst, Lord Chancellor, were present.

Harold Evans married Tina Brown on 19 August 1981 at Grey Gardens, East Hampton, Long Island, USA. Best Man: Ben Bradlee, editor of the *Washington Post*, whose summer home Grey Gardens was.

David Frost married Lynne Frederick, widow of Peter Sellers, on 25 January 1981. Best Man: Michael Rosenberg.

Bob Geldof married Paula Yates on 21 June 1986 in Las Vegas. No Best Man.

George VI (then Duke of York) married Lady Elizabeth Bowes-Lyon on 26 April 1923 in Westminster Abbey, the first royal wedding to have taken place there since that of Richard II to Princess Anne of Bohemia some five hundred and forty years previously. Best Man: David, Prince of Wales (later Edward VIII and Duke of Windsor).

William Ewart Gladstone married Catherine Glynne on 25 July 1839 at Hawarden Parish Church, Cheshire. Best Man: Francis Doyle, Gladstone's fellow Old Etonian, Oxonian and Member of Parliament. This was a double wedding with Mary Glynne and George, Lord Lyttleton.

Cary Grant married Betsy Drake (his third wife) on Christmas Day 1949. Best Man: Howard Hughes, the millionaire recluse.

Thomas Hardy married Emma Lavinia Gifford on 17 September 1874 at St Peter's, Paddington, London. No Best Man. Witnesses: Dr E.H. Gifford (Bride's uncle), Walter Gifford (brother) and Sarah Williams, the daughter of Hardy's landlady.

Thomas Hardy married Florence Emily Dugdale on 10 February 1914 at 8 am at Enfield Parish Church, Middlesex. No Best Man. In the presence only of Henry Hardy (brother), Florence's father and her youngest sister.

George Harrison married Patti Boyd in January 1966 at Epsom Register Office. Best Man: Brian Epstein, the Beatles' manager.

George Harrison married Olivia Arias in September 1978 at Henley-on-Thames Register Office. The

Bride's parents were the witnesses and the only guests. No Best Man.

Elton John married Renate Blauel on 14 February 1984 in a tiny church in Darling Point, Sydney, Australia, four days after he proposed to her in an Indian restaurant. Best Man: John Reid, Elton's manager.

Simon Le Bon married Yasmin Parvenah on 27 December 1985 at Oxford Register Office. No Best Man.

John Lennon married Yoko Ono on 20 March 1969 in Gibralter. They began the day in Paris, where they chartered a jet and flew to the rock for the ceremony, returning in the afternoon. The Bride wore a white knitted minidress, big floppy hat, sunglasses, knee-length woolly socks and tennis shoes. The Groom wore white slacks, jacket and tennis shoes. No Best Man. The two witnesses were the Beatles' personal assistant, Peter Brown, and David Nutter, a photographer friend.

John McEnroe married Tatum O'Neal on 1 August 1986 at St Dominic's Roman Catholic Church, Oyster Bay, New York. No Best Man. Ushers were McEnroe's doubles partner Peter Fleming and brothers Mark McEnroe and Junior Davis Cup team member Patrick McEnroe.

Paul McCartney married Linda Eastman on 12 March 1969. Best Man: Mike McCartney, the Groom's brother, better known as Mike McGear of The Scaffold pop group. The train carrying the

Best Man broke down with the result that he was extremely late for the ceremony, but as there was no other wedding booked for later in the day all was well.

Roger McGough married Hilary Clough in 1987. Best Man: Brian Patten, fellow Beat Poet.

Prince Michael of Kent married Baroness Marie-Christine von Riebnitz on 30 June 1978 in a civil ceremony in the Town Hall, Vienna. No Best Man.

Roger Moore married Doorn van Steyn on 9 December 1946 at Wandsworth Register Office, London. He was nineteen. She was an ice-skater/actress. They divorced in 1953. On 6 July 1953, Moore married Dorothy Squires. Best Man: Joe Latona of Warren, Latona, Sparkes, a comedy knockabout act. Then on 11 April 1969 he married for the third time, to Luisa Mattioli. He was forty-one, she thirty-two. Best Man: Kenneth More, who precipitated the wedding; Dorothy Squires would not divorce Moore, and he and Mattioli lived together. At the 1968 British Film Academy Awards, Kenneth More referred to Mattioli on television as Roger Moore's wife. Dorothy Squires sued him and Granada Television.

Lord Louis Mountbatten married Edwina Ashley in 1922. Best Man: David, Prince of Wales (later Edward VIII and Duke of Windsor).

Lieutenant Philip Mountbatten, R.N. married Princess Elizabeth on 20 November 1947 in Westminster Abbey. Best Man: Marquis of Milford Haven.

Horatio Nelson married Fanny Nesbit on 11 March 1787 at Nevis, West Indies, in the principal reception room at Montpelier. Ceremony performed by Rev William Jones, Rector of the Parish of St John and St Thomas. No Best Man, but Prince William Henry was present, and spoke of Fanny as 'the principal favourite of the island'.

Hazel O'Connor married Kurt Blippert on 23 July 1988 on a beach at Venice, California. Best Man: David Rappaport, the dwarf actor. The Bride was thirty-three, the Groom twenty-six. A Hare Krishna ceremony to which the Bride wore a twenty pound, secondhand, crinoline dress and black ballet shoes. The Groom wore a dark suit with the trousers rolled up. She was given away by David Wakeling, ex-The Beat, who wore a dark jacket, white shirt and shorts, black socks and boots.

Angus Ogilvy married Princess Alexandra on 24 April 1963 in Westminster Abbey. Best Man: Peregrine Fairfax. Chief bridesmaid: Princess Anne. They were the first royal couple ever to have a shop wedding list. When Kensington councillors collected sixty guineas (£63.00) for a wedding gift and rang Kensington Palace to ask what the couple would like, they received the practical reply, 'Could we have the money to choose something we really want?'

Dr David Owen married Deborah Schabert on 28 December 1968 at St James Episcopal Church, Long Island, USA. Best Man: Malcolm Borthwick.

Sean Penn married Madonna in August 1985 at a

115

three million dollar beach house in Malibu hired for the occasion. Best Man: Timothy Hutton. (Prior to the wedding, Penn had kept the identity of his Best Man a secret from the press. The bookies' favourites for the job had been actors Tom Cruise and Matt Dillon.)

Captain Mark Philips married Princess Anne on 14 November 1973 in Westminster Abbey. Groomsman: Captain Eric Grounds, adjutant of the Queen's Dragoon Guards.

Elvis Presley had two Best Men at his marriage to Priscilla Beaulieu. They were Joe Esposito and Marty Lacker.

Ronald Reagan married Nancy Davis in 1950 at the Little Brown Church in San Fernando Valley, California. The matron-of-honour and Best Man were Ardis and William Holden.

Franklin Delano Roosevelt married Eleanor Roosevelt on 17 March 1905 on East 76th Street, New York. Best Man: Lathrop Brown.

Peter Sellers married four times. His first marriage, to Ann Howe, took place on 15 September 1951 at Caxton Hall, Westminster, London. At his second, to Britt Ekland on 19 February 1964 at Guildford Register Office, Surrey, he had two Best Men, actors David Lodge and Graham Stark. On 24 August 1970 he married Miranda Quarry, the stepdaughter of Lord Mancroft. Best Man: Bert Mortimer, his chauffeur, valet and companion. Ms Quarry's bridesmaids were Tabitha and Thomasina, two Pekingese dogs. On 18

February 1977, Sellers married Lynne Frederick in a five minute ceremony in Paris. No Best Man.

George Bernard Shaw married Charlotte Payne-Townshend on 1 June 1898 at West Strand Register Office, London. No Best Man, but Graham Wallas and Henry Salt were present. Shaw had written only two weeks earlier: 'If I were to get married myself, I should resort to some country where the marriage law is somewhat less than five centuries out of date.'

Mel Smith married Pamela Gay-Rees on 30 April 1988. Best Man: Griff Rhys Jones, Smith's collaborator on the television comedy series *Not the Nine O'Clock News* and *Alas Smith and Jones*.

Ringo Starr married Maureen Cox on 11 February 1965 at Caxton Hall, Westminster. Best Man: Brian Epstein, the Beatles' manager. Bride and Groom met at The Cavern in Liverpool. Divorced in 1975. On 28 April 1981, he married Barbara Bach at Marylebone Register Office, London. No Best Man.

David Steel married Judy McGregor in October 1962. Best Man: Michael Steel, the Groom's brother.

Robert Louis Stevenson married Fanny Osbourne, an American divorcée with two children, on 19 May 1880 in San Francisco. Dora Williams, a friend who attended the wedding, was, in Stevenson's description, 'my guardian angel and our Best Man rolled into one'.

Elizabeth Taylor has married seven times:
    1 Conrad Hilton, 1950.

2 Michael Wilding, film star, on 21 February 1952 at Caxton Hall, Westminster. Best Man: Herbert Wilcox, film producer. He and his wife, Anna Neagle, signed the register

3 Mike Todd, on 2 February 1957.

4 Eddie Fisher, singer, on 13 May 1959 in a Jewish ceremony at the Beth-Shalom Temple. Best Man: Mike Todd Jr, her late husband's eldest son.

5 Richard Burton, on 16 March 1964 at the Ritz-Carlton Hotel in Montreal. Best Man: Robert Wilson. They were married by a Unitarian minister. No marriage licence is required in Quebec. Only ten guests attended. They divorced, but later remarried.

6 Richard Burton, October 1975.

7 Senator John Warner, 1976.

Pierre Trudeau married Margaret Sinclair in 1971. Best Man: Charles Trudeau, the Groom's brother.

Kenneth Tynan married Kathleen Halton on 30 June 1967. Four days before the wedding, they discovered that guilty parties in divorces (which both of them were) could not marry in New York State until three years had elapsed. Therefore they drove in a rented Cadillac to Englewood, New Jersey with Steve Vinaver, Penelope Gilliatt and matron-of-honour Marlene Dietrich. When they arrived in Englewood, the Judge asked them, 'You sure you want to go through all this marriage baloney?' No Best Man.

Orson Welles married Virginia Nicholson on 23 December 1934 at the home of her godparents in

East Orange, New Jersey. Best Man: Dr Maurice Bernstein. On 7 September 1943, Welles married Rita Hayworth at Santa Monica Superior Court. Best Man: Joseph Cotten.

Rebecca West married Henry Andrews. Best Man: Douglas Woodruff of *The Times*, later editor of *The Tablet*.

The Duke of Windsor married Mrs Wallis Simpson on 3 June 1937 at Candé in France. Best Man: Major Edward Dudley 'Fruity' Metcalfe. When Metcalfe married, his Best Man was Lord Louis Mountbatten.

Terry Wogan married Helen Joyce on 24 April 1965 at the Church of Refuge, Rathmines, Dublin. Best Man: Brian Wogan, the Groom's brother.

X
CHECKLISTS

An Engagement is Announced

1 *Advertisement* in 'Forthcoming Marriages' column(s)
2 *Engagement Party*
   Date
   Time
   Place
   Invitations
3 *The Wedding*
   Date
   Time
   Place
   Dress: formal or informal?
   Number of Guests
   Invitations: engage printer
      send out six weeks before wedding
4 *Wedding List*
   Consult department store
      or
   Compile your own
   Send out when requested by guests
5 *Best Man and Ushers* (up to five) to be appointed by the Groom
6 *Bridesmaids and pageboys* to be appointed by the Bride
7 *Best Man to meet chief bridesmaid*
8 *Transport*

Separate vehicles needed for going to ceremony
for:
      A Bride's mother and attendants
      B Bride and Bride's father
Separate vehicles needed after ceremony for:
      A Bride and Groom
      B Attendants
      C Bride's parents
9 *Invite minister to reception*

Stag Night

The Best Man should:
      Ask Groom where he would like to go
      Find out exact number of guests
      Book venue
      Stay sober
      Make sure Groom gets home in one piece

Eleventh Hour

The Best Man should:
1 *Attend fitting* of the wedding suits
2 *Arrange car or taxi* for going-away
3 *Attend church rehearsal* if required by minister
4 *Get service sheets*

Wedding Day

The Best Man should remember:
1 *To wake Groom*
2 *Buttonholes*
3 *Time of leaving for ceremony*
4 *Time of ceremony*
5 *To pick up Telemessages*
6 *Wedding Ring*
7 *Banns Certificate*

or
Common Licence
or
Special Licence
8 *Going-away clothes*
9 *Honeymoon baggage*
10 *Toiletries*
11 *Money*
12 *Foreign money*
13 *Passport*
14 *Driving licence*
15 *Insurance*
16 *Tickets*
17 *Innoculation certificates*
18 *Service sheets for Ushers*
19 *Fees for*
　marriage
　clergyman
　organist
　bellringers
　choir
　verger
20 *Phone numbers of local taxi companies*
21 *The Speeches - don't leave them behind!*
22 *Help arrange group photograph outside church*

Reception

The Best Man should be sure to remember:
1 *The names of*:
　Bride's mother
　Bride's father
　Groom's mother
　Groom's father
　Minister

    Bridesmaids
    Ushers
    Groom's brothers and sisters
    Bride's brothers and sisters
    VIPs

2 *To give Master of Ceremonies the names of the speakers*
    Bride's father
    Groom
    Best Man

3 *To tell Master of Ceremonies the time speeches should start*
4 *The time Bride and Groom go off to change*
5 *The time going-away transport should be ready*
6 *The going-away time*

Items for Decorating Going-away Car

1 *Old shoes for rear bumper*
2 *Sign saying 'Just Married'*
3 *Horseshoes*
4 *Tin Cans*
5 *String for attaching above items*
6 *Shaving Cream*
7 *Coal*
8 *White ribbon for bonnet*
9 *Confetti*
10 *Rice*
11 *Rose petals*
12 *Straw*

USEFUL ADDRESSES

Marriage licence enquiries:
The Vicar General and Master of Faculties
1 The Sanctuary
London SW1

Special licence enquiries:
The Registrar of the Court of Faculties
1 The Sanctuary
London SW1

For details of *The Complete Rite of Marriage with Nuptial Mass:*
The Catholic Truth Society
40 Eccleston Square
London SW1

For details of *To Love And To Cherish:*
The British Humanist Association
13 Prince of Wales Terrace
London W8

INDEX